CONTENTS

WHO WANTS TO BE A MILLIONAIRE?

Don't all shout at once! If you're looking for ways to make money, you've come to the right place. This book is stuffed full with more money-making schemes than a whole series of *Dragon's Den*. From quick ways to make money right now to glamorous jobs you could do in the future, you'll find tons of great ideas that will set you off on your journey to making your first million.

If you want to find out how playing videogames can help you win the jackpot and planting seeds can make your savings grow, turn the page and let's start making some money!

GET CRAFTY

If you want to get creative about how you make your cash, check out the ideas in this section. You'll find some great money-making schemes that will let you show off your artistic talents at the same time.

This section will tell you how to:

- Get in credit by making greeting cards for cash
- Create glittering profits by making and selling jewellery
- Make money by designing your own T-shirts
- Clean up cash-wise by making soap and other bath-time treats
- Create candles you can sell as the perfect Christmas gift
- Make money by baking your own biscuits

Are you ready? It's time to make more than just money!

How to make cards into cash

Want to wish someone luck or tell them to get well soon? Send a secret Valentine message or just say "Happy Birthday"? For every occasion, there's a greeting card to match. By making and selling your own cards, you can make every day a "Happy Money" day!

Choose the occasion

First of all, decide what kind of greeting card you want to make. Valentine's Day, Mother's Day, Christmas – all these occasions sell lots of cards, but they only come round once a year. It's a good idea to create a range of designs for different occasions that your customers can choose from. Then you can change the cards that you sell depending on the time of year – Easter cards in spring, Christmas cards in winter and birthday cards all year round!

Get creative

You don't need to be a top-drawer artist to make your own greeting cards. Be crafty – you can create great cards using craft materials, computer software or even just a digital camera. The most important thing is to come up with an imaginative design to make your cards stand out from the crowd.

Visit shops that sell greeting cards to check out the competition. You could ask the person who runs the shop what their bestselling card is. This might help you to come up with ideas for your own design.

How to make a greeting card

Follow these tips to help you create some cool-looking cards.

1. First make sure you've got the right materials. Thin cardboard for your cards and envelopes to put them in are essential! You might also need a pencil, a stencil, glue and scissors depending on how you decide to make your card.

2. Think up a design that fits the occasion. You don't want a Christmas tree on a Valentine's card or a Mother's Day card with a picture of a dad! Here are some design ideas for different occasions:

• Birthday — pictures of cartoon dogs or cats would make a great design for any animal-lover's birthday. If you want to make some sporty birthday cards, you could cut the shapes of footballs, rugby ball and cricket bats out of felt to stick on to your card.

• Valentine's Day — heart-shapes are a favourite Valentine design, but think of ways to make your cards stand out from the crowd. How about a cartoon bee with the message "Bee Mine"? Use your imagination.

• Christmas — Santa Claus, sleigh bells, snowmen, shepherds, stockings and stars. If you stick to some snowy ideas that begin with the letter "S" you'll probably make a great Christmas card!

3. You might need to get crafty to create your design. You could cut pieces of coloured felt into shapes, and glue on buttons, feathers, sequins and ribbons.

9

4. If you don't want to get crafty, you could take fun and funny pictures with a digital camera, cut out cool snaps from your favourite magazine or use a computer program to create a design for the front of your cards.

Deliver the profit

Once you've made your greeting cards, it's time to get selling.

• School fetes and craft fairs are a good place to showcase your cards.

• Work out the price you want to charge for each card. Firstly, add up the money you have spent on the materials. Then add a charge for the time you spent making it – this might be £4 for an hour's work. Now take this total and double it to give you your price – this doubling is your mark-up and will help you make a profit.

• You could also visit gift shops in your local area. Take samples of your cards along to show the owner and ask if they'd like to sell them. They'll want to take a cut of the profits too, so make sure you negotiate a good deal.

• Tell all your family and friends. If your cards look cool, you will end up with an avalanche of orders.

How to make and sell jewellery

All that glitters isn't gold, but selling jewellery can put some serious sparkle into your bank account. Don't panic, you won't need to break into the Tower of London to steal the Crown Jewels! Here's how you can design and make your own jewellery to sell instead.

Decide on a design

Earrings, necklaces, bangles, bracelets — choose what type of jewellery you want to make. Do you want to make something that looks sleek and sophisticated or create a fantastic and bling-tastic design?

To help you decide, do some market research. Ask your friends what type of jewellery they like to buy. You could also pop into a shop and ask a jeweller what designs they sell the most of. Don't copy these though — choosing a unique look for the jewellery you make will make your designs one of a kind.

Get the right kit

You can find all the equipment and materials you need to make your own jewellery in craft shops, charity shops and even around your own home. Your jewellery making kit could include:

- Scissors
- Elastic thread
- A needle
- Beads
- A work board (like an old chopping board)
- Masking tape

Beady eye-catching bracelets

Beads come in lots of different colours, textures and shapes and can be used to make stunningly beautiful bracelets.

1. Measure out a length of elastic thread so it can fit around your wrist. Make sure you leave some extra thread so you can tie the bracelet together at the end and still fit it around your wrist.

2. Stick one end of the thread to your work board with masking tape. Thread your needle with the other end, and use your needle to go through the holes in the beads to string them on to the thread.

3. Think about the shapes, colours and textures of the beads you choose. Mix them together to create a cool-looking design.

4. When your thread is full, peel off the masking tape. Knot the ends of the thread together and your bracelet is ready to wear!

You can also use beads to make nifty necklaces and elegant earrings. If your budget doesn't stretch to buying new beads from craft shops, check out charity shops and jumble sales instead. You could buy cheap old necklaces and cut them up to get at the beads.

Shiny happy profits

Now you need to show off your jewellery and start making money.

• Work out the price you want to charge for each piece — add up the money you have spent making it, pay yourself for the time you took, and double this total to give you your price.

• Presentation counts. You could invest in gift boxes to display each piece of jewellery. Remember to add the cost of these to the price you charge.

• Advertise! Let the most stylish girl in your school wear some of your jewellery for free. This will show off your designs and soon all her friends will want to buy them too.

• You could also sell your jewellery at craft fairs, school fetes or even online.

How to design T-shirts

Designing your own T-shirts is a great way to freshen up your wardrobe and make some money at the same time. Sell the T-shirts you make to raise some extra cash or keep them yourself to get a cool new T-shirt without splashing any cash.

Styles, slogan, logos and designs

From funny slogans to band logos, funky prints to cool cartoons — the only limit to what you can put on a T-shirt is your imagination. First, decide which T-shirt designing technique to use. You could:

• Use an iron-on transfer to create a cool-looking T-shirt. Create a design on your computer or upload a fun photo that would look great on the front of a tee. Print this out on to special T-shirt transfer paper. Place the transfer face down on the front of the T-shirt and iron it on — ask an adult to help you.

• Screen print a T-shirt. You'll need special equipment to do this, but it can create some eye-catching designs. But be careful — it can be a messy business!

• Get someone else to make your T-shirt for you. If you don't fancy getting your hands dirty, this is a good technique to try! Lots of online stores will let you create your own design and then make the T-shirt for you. Some stores will even you sell your T-shirts too, but they'll take a cut of the profits as well.

• Tie-dye a T-shirt to create a one-of-a-kind design.

How to tie-dye a T-shirt

You will need:

- A plain T-shirt (any colour you like!)
- Pots of fabric dye (pick colours that will go well with your T-shirt)
- A bucket
- Rubber gloves
- A stick or long-handled spoon
- Elastic bands
- Old newspapers

1. Cover your work surface with newspapers to make sure you don't dye the kitchen table too!

2. Use a bucket to mix the dye. Wear rubber gloves and follow the instructions that came with the dye carefully.

3. Lay the T-shirt out on a flat surface. You're now ready to create your tie-dye design.

To make stripes...

- Fold the bottom edge of the T-shirt up by about 5 cm.

- Now take the new bottom edge and fold 5 cm of this under the T-shirt.

- Keep folding backwards and forwards until the T-shirt looks like a paper fan.

- Wrap elastic bands around the T-shirt, spacing these out every 3 cm.

To make circles...

- Pick up the centre of the T-shirt and lift it up until the whole T-shirt is hanging in the air.

- Gather together the dangling material and then put an elastic band around the T-shirt just below where you are holding it.

- Now add more elastic bands around the T-shirt – each one should be about 4 cm apart.

To make a spiral...

- Grab the centre of the T-shirt and slowly start to spin it so the T-shirt twists around.

- Twist the T-shirt up until it's in a tight bundle.

- Now wrap two elastic bands around the T-shirt so that it keeps the spiral shape you have made.

4. Now you can dip your tied-up T-shirt in the dye! Use the stick or long-handled spoon to stir it around. Don't forget to follow the instructions on the dye to time this part right.

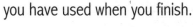

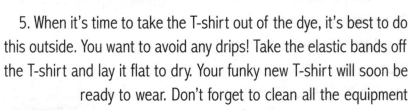

5. When it's time to take the T-shirt out of the dye, it's best to do this outside. You want to avoid any drips! Take the elastic bands off the T-shirt and lay it flat to dry. Your funky new T-shirt will soon be ready to wear. Don't forget to clean all the equipment you have used when you finish.

How to make lotions and potions

Making soaps and moisturizing lotions can help you to clean up cash-wise. If you can sell your luxurious bath-time treats, it'll be your bank account that ends up smelling sweet.

Multicoloured soap shop

Here's how you can brighten up any bathroom with home-made soap. You will need:

• Clear bars of glycerine soap (not coloured!) – you can buy these from pharmacists or online
• A microwave
• A kitchen knife
• A plastic jug (that you can safely use in the microwave)
• Small bottles of food colouring (any colours you like!)
• Essential oils (rose, lavender or any other scents that you like)
• Small silicone jelly moulds in seashell, star or animal shapes
• Cellophane paper

Important! Make sure an adult helps you to make your soap, as the melted soap will be very hot!

1. Cut up the soap into small squares. Put them in the jug.

2. Now put the jug in the microwave. Turn the microwave on a medium heat until the soap is completely melted.

3. Ask an adult to help you take the jug out of the microwave. Quickly, add a quarter of a teaspoon of food colouring and stir. Choose a colour that will match your essential oil, such as red for rose.

4. Now add half a teaspoon of your essential oil and stir the mixture again. Make sure you mix it well, but don't take too long or the melted soap might start to set.

5. Pour the melted soap mixture into the jelly moulds and leave to set overnight.

6 When the soap is set, press it out of the mould and wrap it in cellophane paper. It's ready to sell!

Make a bomb!

If your home-made soap makes a splash, you could try your hand at making bath bombs and body lotions. You can buy kits to make these from craft shops. Why not make a selection of bath-time treats to create the ultimate pampering gift pack? You could sell these as the perfect present for family and friends.

True story of bath-time tycoons

If your business selling bath-time treats takes off, you might end up a multi-millionaire! That's what happened to Mark and Mo Constantine when they set up their company Lush in 1994.

Mark and Mo started selling soaps, bath bombs and moisturizing creams in a small shop in Dorset, but there are now hundreds of Lush stores all around the world. The soaps, bath bombs and moisturizers they sell help make the company millions of pounds in profits. So what's the secret behind their success?

Looking good, smelling great!

Presentation matters. With sensational-smelling soaps and colourful bath-bombs that look like cakes, a trip to a Lush shop is an exciting experience for any shopper. Think about how you can make the bath-time treats you create look and smell as sweet. Putting extra care into the way you present your product can help to increase your profits!

How to make candles

Looking for a bright idea to earn a few quid? How about making your own candles to sell?

How to make beeswax candles

Beeswax candles can make a room smell like honey — the perfect gift for anyone with a sweet tooth. To make them, you will need:

• Rectangular sheets of beeswax in different colours (you can buy these from most craft shops)

• Pre-waxed candle wicks (you can buy these from most craft shops too!)

• A ruler

• Scissors

• A cutting board

• Plastic wrapping paper

• Ribbons

1. Lay a sheet of beeswax on top of the cutting board.

2. Place a candle wick along the end of one of the short edges of the beeswax sheet. The bottom of the wick should meet the end of the sheet, and the top should stick out 1 cm at the other end.

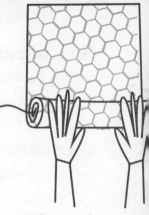

3. Gently press the wick into the wax. Then slowly roll the sheet around wick. Make sure you roll the sheet as tightly as you can and keep both ends of the candle even. If the beeswax is too stiff to roll, try using a hairdryer to soften it. Don't make it too hot though or the wax might melt!

4. When you finish rolling the candle, gently press the edge of the sheet into the candle to seal the seam.

5. To add some artistic touches to your candle, you could cut small heart shapes out from another sheet of beeswax and stick these on. Wrap your finished candle in plastic wrapping, tie it with a ribbon bow and it's ready to sell!

Remember to add up the money you have spent on the materials you have used to make the candles. Then add a charge for the time you spent making it – this might be £4 for an hour's work. Now take this total and double it to give you your price – this doubling is your mark-up and will help you make a good profit.

How to bake your own dough

Are you a junior Jamie Oliver? Selling the tasty treats that you bake can be a great way of making some cash. You can set up a stall to sell your biscuits or cakes at a school fair, a village fete, or even from your garden gate. Here's a tempting recipe to get you started.

How to make gingerbread stars

To bake twenty of these delicious biscuits, you will need:

- 350 g self-raising flour
- 200 g of brown sugar
- 125 g of butter or margarine
- 4 tablespoons of golden syrup
- 2 teaspoons of ground ginger
- 1 teaspoon of bicarbonate of soda
- 1 egg
- A large bowl
- A sieve
- A wooden spoon
- A rolling pin
- A knife
- A baking tray
- A star-shaped cutter

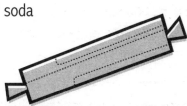

1. Sieve the flour, ginger and bicarbonate of soda into the bowl.

2. Cut the butter into small chunks and add it to the mixture. Use your fingers to work it in and make sure it's evenly spread.

3. Crack the egg and mix it in with the wooden spoon. Stir in the sugar and syrup, and then knead the dough with your fingers.

4. Roll out the dough evenly until it's about 5 mm thick. Now use your star cutter to cut out the biscuit shapes.

5. Place your biscuit stars on a greased baking tray. Make sure you spread them out as they'll get bigger as they bake.

6. Ask an adult to help you put the tray in the oven and then bake at 190°C/Gas mark 5 for 15 minutes. Watch the biscuits carefully — when they turn golden brown they're ready!

7. Ask an adult to help you take the baking tray out of the oven.

Warning — it will be very hot! Leave for five minutes to let the biscuits go firm then place on a wire rack to cool.

8. You could use icing to decorate your biscuits or just sell them as they are. Either way they'll taste delicious!

The biscuit bottom line

When you are selling your biscuits, there are lots of things you can do to maximize your profits by charging the right price.

• Work out the total cost of your ingredients. Then divide this by the number of biscuits you have made. This will tell you how much each biscuit has cost to make.

• Now think about what you can charge for each biscuit to give you a healthy profit. Remember, if you try to sell the biscuits too cheaply you won't make enough money, but if you charge too much nobody will want to buy them anyway.

• If your biscuits don't start to sell, have a special offer to drum up interest – buy two biscuits, get one free! Drop your price near the end of day to get rid of any biscuits you have left.

MAKE MONEY WITH YOUR MATES

Think making money sounds like hard work? Think again! There are plenty of ways to have fun with your friends and make money at the same time.

This section will tell you how to:

- Turn the silver screen into gold with your own cinema
- Make money out of music by staging a concert
- Run a quiz night to make a smart profit
- Organize a video-game tournament

If you want to become a money-making star, why not start off by opening your own cinema?

How to run your own cinema

Want to make a blockbuster profit? How about turning your front room into a home cinema? Turn the lights down, break out the popcorn and get ready to find out how.

Flicks hits and misses

Before you start to set up your own picture house, think about all the things you like about going to the cinema. These might be:
- Watching great films on a big screen
- Hanging out with your friends
- Stuffing your face with popcorn

Now think about the things that bug you:
- Sky-high ticket prices
- Rip-off food and drink
- People talking on their phones during the film!

To get people to come to your home cinema, you'll need to give them the things they love and get rid of the things they hate.

Fantastic films

Take a poll of the films your friends want to watch. Pick the top-rated films from this poll and arrange a screening at your house. Borrow Blu-rays or DVDs from the library or record the films if they're on TV.

Great food

You can't have a cinema that doesn't sell popcorn! Here's how to make buckets of this tasty treat in just ten minutes. You will need:

- A large saucepan with a glass lid
- 75 g of popcorn kernels
- 25 g of butter
- 2 tablespoons of sunflower oil
- A pinch of salt

Warning – ask an adult to help you make this recipe.

1. Add the sunflower oil to the saucepan and heat it up. Sprinkle in the popcorn kernels, making sure you swirl them round the pan to coat them evenly in oil.

2. Cover the saucepan with the glass lid and turn the heat down to low. Watch and listen as the kernels start to pop. When the popping stops, take the saucepan off the heat.

3. Melt the butter and add it to the popcorn along with a pinch of salt. Shake well to make sure the butter spreads over every piece. Your popcorn is now ready to sell.

You could make toffee popcorn by adding 40 g of brown sugar and 2 tablespoons of golden syrup to the melted butter. Stir this over a high heat for two minutes and then pour the toffee mixture over the popcorn. Let it cool down before you serve it up. You could sell mini-popcorn portions in paper cups or as a jumbo-sized treat in a jar!

How to stage a concert

If you want to make it in music but can't sing or play an instrument, why not stage your own concert? There's money to be made – some bands make more from playing gigs than from selling CDs.

Step 1 – Find a venue

Ideally, this should be somewhere with a stage and space for lots of people to watch. You probably won't be able to afford to book the 02 arena, but you could see if your village hall is for hire or ask your school if you could stage the concert there instead.

Step 2 – Find the band

Do you want to book a top pop star? Then you'll need to pay them big money. You might be better booking an up-and-coming band in your area. They'll have lots of local fans who want to see them play.

Step 3 – Promote the concert

Make fliers and posters to advertise the concert. Don't forget to include:
- The name of the band (and a picture too!)
- The concert venue
- The date of the show
- The price of tickets and where to buy them

Let local radio stations, newspapers and websites know about the concert. The more mentions it gets, the more chance you have of drawing a crowd.

Step 4 – Sell tickets

Print tickets to sell before the show. That way you'll keep track of how many people are coming and get some money up front. On the night of the concert, sell any left-over tickets on the door. You could charge a bit extra for these to up your profit. Make sure you check how many people the venue is allowed to hold before you print your tickets. Don't let any extra people in!

Step 5 – Stage the show

Ask your friends to help you to run the concert. You'll need someone to look after lighting, sound and stage equipment. Someone else could help selling tickets and refreshments.

Give the band plenty of drinks and snacks and don't forget to give them their share of the profits after they've played. If the concert is a big success, plan another show. Next stop – Wembley Stadium!

How to run a quiz night

Question: What's a fun way to make some cash using only paper, pencils and a microphone? Answer: Running your own quiz night! Read these top tips to organizing a quiz to find out how.

Quiz whiz

You could set up a quiz night at your local youth club. Make it a regular event, the same day and time every week. Create posters and fliers to advertise the quiz night and tell all your friends to come.

Cash for questions

A great quiz needs great questions. You can research these on the internet – lots of websites have lists of ready-prepared quiz questions you can use or you could make up your own.

Choose topics that will interest the people who will come along to your quiz. You could have themed rounds about vampires, Harry Potter or even Manchester United!

Don't make your questions too hard or too easy or your quiz won't be fun to play. Try your questions out on a friend to make sure you've got them right. You could have a round where all the questions are multiple-choice or include a picture quiz where contestants have got to name the celebrities from close-up pictures of their noses!

Points mean prizes

The best way to attract a big crowd to your quiz is to offer attractive prizes. If you charge each person £1 to enter the quiz and 50 people turn up, you could give away a £20 prize to the winning team and still make a tidy profit.

As well as having a prize for the team who gets the most points, you could also offer a bonus prize for:
- The team who gets every question right in a bonus round.
- The team who gets nearest to a guess the number question. E.g. How tall is the world's tallest man?
- The team with the funniest name.

The more prizes your quiz has, the more chances teams will have to win. This will keep people coming back week after week.

Make it fun

On the night of the quiz, make sure there are lots of chairs and tables for the teams to sit at. You'll need plenty of pencils and paper as well so they can write down their answers. Hand these out when you collect each team's entry fee.

If one of your friends is good at making everyone laugh, ask them to be the quizmaster. They'll make it an event to remember!

How to organize a video-game tournament

Do lots of your friends love playing video games? Are you always competing to see who can beat the rest? Organizing your own video-game tournament can help settle these arguments and give you a chance of making money.

Find a place

Choose a place where you can all get together to play. This might be somebody's front room or basement den. You'll need comfy chairs, a game console, TV and enough drinks and snacks to keep everyone happy.

Choose the game

Pick a video game that everyone likes to play. Some games work better than others in a tournament situation. Fighting, racing and football games let you compete one-on-one with your friends.

Agree the rules

You could organize your tournament as a knockout with the winner of each contest going through to the next round. Otherwise set up a league with each player getting points for a win. Remember to set a time limit for each game to stop the people watching getting bored and make sure that everyone has a chance to play.

Pick a prize

For the ultimate champion, you've got to have a prize. If you charge each of your friends an entry fee, the winner could take home the lot — or, if you want to make a profit, you can keep a cut for yourself and give away the rest. With plenty of practise, you'll soon be ready to take on the professionals. Check out page 119 to find out more.

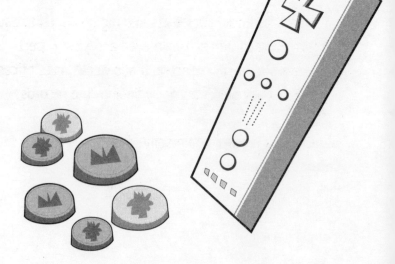

FINDING AND COLLECTING

Want to find a fortune? Fancy collecting your way to a million-pound bank account? Maybe you just want to bargain your way to a better deal? Well, keep on reading to find out how.

This section will tell you how to:

- Search for ancient artefacts and dig up buried treasure
- Turn yourself into an eagle-eyed antiques' expert
- Create a fantastic collection that's worth loads of cash
- Make money out of music by finding rare records

Get ready. It's time to dig up some dosh!

How to find buried treasure

Money doesn't grow on trees, but you can find lost treasures by looking underground — lost coins, ancient jewellery and other hidden prizes.

How to use a metal detector

A metal detector can help you find buried treasure. If you haven't got one, you can download an app that turns your phone into a metal detector for free!

1. Turn on your metal detector. Holding it by the handle, sweep the search coil at the base of the detector over the area you are searching. Remember to keep the search coil close to the ground, but don't touch the ground itself.

2. Move the search coil slowly from side to side and keep track of where you have searched. Move forward slowly and listen carefully to the sound your metal detector is making. When the detector is close to metal, you will hear a change in the sound it makes.

3. When you think you have found something, dig carefully until you uncover your find. Place your discovery in a plastic bag to keep it safe. Make a note of the exact spot where you found the treasure.

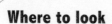

Where to look

There are many places where you can discover lost treasures from the past. Here are some of the best places to look:

• Fields — If a field has recently been ploughed by a farmer, this can bring hidden treasures closer to the surface. In 2007, a young boy and his father treasure-hunting in a field in Yorkshire found a hoard of ancient Viking coins worth more than £1 million!

• Woods — Searching on old footpaths and tracks in woodland can turn up old coins and objects left behind by earlier travellers.

• Beaches — The best time to go treasure-hunting on a beach is after a storm, when interesting finds can be washed up. Two treasure-hunters discovered more than 900 medieval silver pennies hidden under the sand on Llanddona beach in Wales.

• Gardens — If you live in an old house or have a friend that does, you can search for lost treasures in the garden. The older the house, the greater chance you have of finding ancient treasures. In 2004, a man digging in his back garden dug up a pot filled with 20,000 Roman coins!

Make sure you get permission from whoever owns the land you're searching on before you start looking for treasure. Take whatever you find to your local museum to find out what it's worth. You could get a reward for finding treasure or even get to keep it.

How to spot an antique

If you're cleaning out your attic and spot what seems like an old piece of junk, make sure you take a closer look — it could be a priceless antique! Follow these tips to find out how to tell a million-pound Picasso from a finger painting and a treasured teddy bear from a scruffy soft toy.

Step 1 – Become an antique expert

There are lots of different types of antiques: statues, paintings, silverware, jewellery, even toys! It would be impossible to learn about all of these, so choose the type you're most interested in and find out all you can about it.

Visit museums, art galleries, antique shops or even historic houses. Take a look at the antiques they have on display and read the information about them. This will help you to recognize what a real antique looks like.

You could also go along to an antiques auction to see what sells for the most money. Make sure you don't scratch your nose when people are bidding though, else you might end up buying your own antique for a sky-high price!

Look in the library or online for more information about the kinds of antiques you are interested in. Are there any hints about rare pieces that will fetch a fortune or tips about spotting a fake? Doing your homework now can help you spot a prized possession later on.

Step 2 – Get hunting

You might not have antiques hiding in your attic – you might not even have an attic! So, where can you go to find a priceless treasure?

Auctions and antique shops are an obvious place to start, but you won't find any bargains that will help you to make a million there. You'll be better off hunting for antiques in less likely places. Check out charity shops and car boot sales to see if there are any lost gems peeping out amongst the old tat – use the detective skills below to find out how to spot these!

If you have got an attic (or somewhere your family dumps all its old stuff!) have a rummage around. That hideous lamp that your mum never liked might be worth a fortune to an antique lamp collector.

Step 3 – Use your detective skills

When you find something that might be valuable, you need to use your detective skills to make sure it's a genuine antique. Look at your find with a magnifying glass to uncover clues that can help you.

- If it's a painting, does it have a signature to show who painted it? Google the name to find out more about the artist, and how much the painting might be worth. Make sure it's not a print, which is a copy of the original painting – prints aren't usually very valuable.

- Other kinds of antiques such as furniture, jewellery and silverware can also be signed or marked to show who made them – but these signatures and hallmarks can be faked. Look carefully to see whether the antique really is as old as it seems to be – do any signs of wear and tear look real? If you're not sure, take a picture to show to an expert in an antique shop or museum who might be able to help.

- Even old toys and teddy bears can be antiques. A toy company called Steiff started making teddy bears more than a century ago. Nowadays, some of their teddy bears sell for tens of thousands of pounds. If you find an old teddy, take a look in its ear – a Steiff teddy bear has a metal button there.

In 2010, a collection of antique teddy bears was sold for more than £1 million!

How to collect a fortune

Collecting stamps, comic books, Pokemon cards or even crisp packets can set you on the path to collecting a fortune. Take a look at these top tips on some of the best things to collect.

Get booked up

Have you got an old copy of *Harry Potter and the Philosopher's Stone* sitting on your bookshelf? Take a closer look – it could be worth up to £20,000! That's what a hardback edition of the book from the very first print run sold for at auction in 2011 – only 500 copies were printed. Here's how to spot a copy of this book:

1. First of all, look on the imprint page – this is the left-hand page at the start of the book which tells you who wrote and published it. Can you see the name Joanne Rowling instead of J K Rowling?

2. Can you find a line of ten numbers running from 10 down to 1 on the imprint page? If you can, this tells you the book is an edition from the very first print run.

3. Finally, look at page 53. Does the word "wand" appear twice on Harry's shopping list for Diagon Alley? If you can find this misprint, then you might have found yourself a fortune!

Books by some authors are worth more than others, but if you start a book collection you'll have more fun collecting books by writers you love. Remember, the better shape a book is in, the more valuable it'll be to a book collector, so look out for first editions in tip-top condition. Hardback books should have a dust jacket and if you can find a signed copy, that'll make it worth even more. Go along to an author signing to increase the value of your collection.

Make a superhero profit

Who's the ultimate superhero. Batman or Superman? Spider-Man or Iron Man? Who has the coolest powers? Who's the strongest? And whose comic book would make you the most money?

• BAM! Detective Comics #27 — the first comic book to feature Batman — was sold for over a million dollars in 2010.

• WHAM! Spider-Man's first appearance in the comic Amazing Fantasy #15 made $1.1 million at auction.

- KA-POW! Superman's very first adventure in Action Comics #1 sold for $1.5 million!

To create your own priceless comic book collection, you could:

- Ask your mum, dad, brother, sister, aunties and uncles if they have any old comics hidden away that you could have.
- Hunt through boxes of old comics in charity shops or school fairs to find any hidden gems.
- Search for comics that feature the first appearances of a famous superhero or cunning super-villain.
- Collect the first issues of any exciting new comic books — maybe one day they'll be worth as much as the very first Superman or Batman comics!

True story of a toy-tycoon

Jeremy Greene started collecting toys as a teenager. He didn't realize that fifty years later his collection would be worth £30 million! His love of trains led him to collect vintage train sets, and he built up a collection of thousands of toy trains, railway stations and figures filling the basement of his house. His collection included some toys that were more than 150 years old.

Treasured toys

Choose a toy and start building up a toy treasure trove!

• Toy cars made by Corgi, Dinky or Matchbox can make a tidy profit. A model of James Bond's Aston Martin with machine guns, pop-up bullet shield and ejector seat which cost 2½p in 1960 is now worth £350.

• If you like dolls, then collecting Barbies could net you a stylish sum. The first Barbie ever made with all her accessories and in her original box was sold for over £2,000 on eBay.

Keep an eye out for old toys at school fetes and second-hand shops. Before you buy, check the toy still works and doesn't have any bits missing. If the toy is still in its original box, this can add to its value.

How to make a record profit

How do you listen to music? On your iPod, or mobile phone? Well, some people still like to listen to old-fashioned records, and this can help you to make a sweet-sounding stash of cash!

Top five tips

You can find stacks of old albums and singles piled up in charity shops. However, most of these tatty 12 inches won't be worth much. You need to keep your eyes open for the tunes that will appeal to a real record collector. Follow these top five tips to help you:

1. Look out for records by singers and bands with lots of fans. The more people who like a band, the more people who will want to collect their records!

2. If you can find a record the band or singer made before they become famous, it might be worth even more. Before The Beatles made it big, they were called The Quarrymen and recorded a song called "That'll Be The Day". Only one copy of this record exists and record collecting experts say it's worth over £100,000!

3. Rare records can bring in the cash. Picture discs, coloured vinyl, promo singles, gold discs — dig through piles of records to look for anything unusual. Music from the children's TV show The Clangers came out in a record with a knitted sleeve!

4. Some people even collect records where the song titles are spelled wrong on the sleeve! Books, magazines and websites about record collecting can help you find the rarest records to look for.

5. If you find a record that you think might be worth a fortune, check out its wear and tear. Only records in the very best condition go for the biggest prices. There's only one mark which will add more money to your find — the singer's signature.

OPPORTUNITY KNOCKS

A smart money-maker can spot an opportunity to make some cash at a hundred paces. If you want to take every chance to make a quick profit, check out these ideas.

This section will tell you how to:

- Get creative with face paints to make a fast profit
- Start a craze that will get your playground buzzing
- Add some fizz to your finances with a lemonade stand
- Become an entertainer at kids' parties and bring in the cash
- House-sit for friends and neighbours
- Sweep snow to make a cool profit

Now get ready to transform your bank account — it's time to get your paints out!

How to paint faces

Want to show off your artistic talents, but bored of painting on paper? Face painting can be a creative way to earn some cash. School fairs and children's parties are great places to start doing this – so get your paintbrush ready!

What you need

To start face painting, you will need:

- A paint palette
- Pots of face paints
- A small paintbrush
- A make-up sponge
- A jar of water
- A hand mirror

Be careful! Don't use any old paints to paint faces. You need special face-painting paints to do this safely. You can buy these from craft shops or online.

Choose the right design

Don't start painting some poor kid's face before you work out what you can actually paint. You don't want to try to paint a butterfly and end up with a squashed spider! Some face-painting kits come with guides showing you how to paint different designs.

When you set up your face-painting stand, have some pictures ready to show the different designs you can paint. Customers will want to choose their favourite. Remember to display a sign that shows your prices too.

How to paint a butterfly face

1. Take your paint palette and add a few drops of pink, yellow, purple and black paint into different sections of the tray. Be careful not to mix the colours.

2. Dip the make-up sponge into the pink paint. Starting from the top inside corner of one eye, use the make-up sponge to make a triangular shape that reaches up to the hairline and back down to the outside corner of the eye. Now do the same for the other eye and you've made the top wings of the butterfly. Don't fill these in yet.

3. To make the bottom wings, start from the inside lower corner of one eye. Use the sponge to make a curved shape that covers the cheek and reaches back up to the outside corner of the eye. Do the same again on the other side and you've got the outline of your butterfly shape.

4. Clean the make-up sponge in the water and then dip it in the purple paint. Dab this around the inside edges of the butterfly wings, leaving a space in the middle of the wings.

5. Clean the sponge again and then dip it in the yellow paint. Dab this to fill in the rest of the butterfly's wings. Make sure you don't get any paint in the eyes of the person who you are painting.

6. Use a paintbrush to trace the outline of the butterfly in black paint. You could add lines and swirls inside the butterfly's wings, too.

7. Finish your face painting by adding the butterfly's antennae. These are two curved black lines that you add above the top of the nose.

Show your customer their face in the mirror and then collect their cash!

True-life story of a make-up tycoon

If you've got the talent to transform someone's look this could make you some serious cash. That's what happened to one amateur make-up artist.

When Lauren Luke sat in her bedroom to film a video tutorial showing how to put on make-up, she didn't realize that she was about to become the most famous make-up artist in the world. The videos she posted up on YouTube showing how to use make-up to get different celebrities' looks soon got millions of hits and made Lauren an internet star.

From her fame, fortune soon followed. As well as her online make-up tutorials, Lauren has launched her own line of cosmetics, written a bestselling book, appeared on TV chat shows and even featured in her own video game. Could you turn your make-up skills into a beautiful career like Lauren?

How to start a craze

From yo-yos to crazy bones, trading cards to diabolos, you can't turn your back for a minute before another new craze has got the playground buzzing. And if you're first on the scene, you can make cash from these crazes.

Find the next big thing

First of all, you need to spot a new craze before it makes it big. Here are some tactics to try:

• Go to a toy fair where toymakers show off their latest toys. See if you can spot toys or games with real playground appeal.

• Look for toys at pocket money prices. The cheaper the toy, the bigger the craze will be – more people will be able to afford it.

• The best crazes can be collectible (Match Attax, Moshi Monster trading cards), or skilful (yo-yos, diabolos), but most of all fun!

• If you've got an older sibling, ask them what playground crazes they remember. Maybe it's time for an old craze to make a comeback!

Negotiate a great deal

Talk the toymaker into selling you a stock of the toys you have chosen at trade prices (the price that a shop would pay). The cheaper you can buy them for, the more profit you'll make when you sell them at full price. Maybe you can negotiate an exclusive deal where you'll be the only person selling the toy in your area. This will cut down on the competition when the craze makes it big.

Build the buzz

You've got your toys, but how are you going to create the craze? Here are some ideas to make everyone want your new toy:

• Give some for free to the coolest kids in school. If they set the style, then they can make your toy cool too.

• If your toy can do tricks like a yo-yo or a diabolo, get someone to show off the tricks. When everyone else sees the toy in action, they'll all want one.

• Spread the word. Tell your friends in nearby schools, cousins on the other side of the country, and post a video on YouTube showing off the toy. If you're lucky you might take the craze nationwide!

True story of a playground tycoon

When Cameron Johnson was 12 years old, he noticed that his sister's friends had a craze for collecting Beanie Babies. He bought his sister's collection of Beanie Babies from her for $100 and sold them himself on eBay for a big profit. In one year he made over $50,000 from selling these toys thanks to the Beanie Baby craze!

Get out at the right time

Every craze must come to an end, so you need to know the right time to move on. You don't want to turn up at school with a bagful of toys to sell when everyone else has started collecting something else instead. If it looks like people are starting to get bored of the craze, get looking for the next big thing instead.

How to set up a lemonade stand

The sun is shining, the weather is hot — it's time to make some money! Setting up a lemonade stand is a great way to make some cash when the temperature's rising. By making refreshing drinks to sell to passers-by, you can soon turn a cool profit.

How to make lemonade

You will need:

- 6 unwaxed lemons
- 280 g of caster sugar
- One litre of ice-cold water
- One litre of chilled sparkling water
- A food processor
- A kitchen knife
- A sieve
- A large mixing bowl
- A serving jug
- Ice cubes

Ask permission before you use the kitchen knife and food processor. You could ask somebody to help you to use these as you make your lemonade.

1. Wash the lemons and then carefully chop each lemon into small pieces using the knife.

2. Add the lemons, sugar and the litre of cold water into the food processor. Blend the mixture until the lemons are finely chopped.

3. Place the sieve over the bowl and pour the mixture into the sieve. Make sure you press through as much of the juice as you can.

4. Add the litre of sparkling water to the bowl and stir. Now add ice cubes to the serving jug and then pour in the mixture from the bowl. You now have your lemonade ready to serve!

Selling the sparkle

Here are some tips to help you to set up a successful lemonade stall:

• Make sure you have everything that you need. As well as your fresh lemonade, you will need a table, a chair, a cool box to keep the lemonade chilled, disposable cups, a rubbish bin and a box to keep the money you make in. You will also need some small coins so that you can give change to anybody who wants to buy your lemonade but hasn't got the exact money.

• Choose a great location to set up your stand. You need to make sure that your stand is somewhere that lots of people will pass by. This could be at the gate to your house or at a friend's house if they live close to a park or somewhere where people go when the weather is hot.

• Set the right price. Work out how many cups of lemonade you have made and decide how much you can charge for each cup. Multiply these two numbers together to work out how much money you could make and then subtract the cost of the ingredients and equipment to give you your potential profit. Remember, increasing the price you charge doesn't mean you will increase your profit if fewer people buy your lemonade. Think carefully about how much people would be willing to pay.

• Advertise. You need to make a large sign for your stand so that people know what you are selling and how much you are charging for your lemonade. Create an attractive design for your sign and choose words that make your lemonade sound appealing such as "delicious" and "fresh".

• Keep an eye on your supplies. If you spot that you are running low, you might need to make a fresh batch of lemonade or buy some more disposable cups. If your lemonade stand is a success, you could also think about selling other things that people might like on a sunny day such as lemonade ice-lollies!

How to entertain at children's parties

If you've got a younger brother or sister and are great at making them laugh, you might be able to make money from your party tricks. Every mum and dad wants their beloved's birthday party to be the best and some will hire an entertainer to keep the kids happy.

Clown around

A clown can be the perfect party entertainer, but you'll need to be funny to keep your audience in stitches. To dress up as a clown, you'll need some brightly-coloured clothes, a wig or funny hat, and a stick-on clown nose. Practise your performance before you arrive at the party. Here are some things you could try:

- Juggling
- Telling jokes
- Riding a unicycle
- Making balloon animals

How to make a balloon dog

Follow these steps to conjure a sausage dog out of a balloon. You'll need a special long balloon that you can twist into shapes — you can buy these from party shops and online. Invest in a pump too to save on your puff!

1. Blow up the balloon until it's halfway inflated and tie a knot in the end.

2. Hold on to the end with the knot and then twist it two or three times to make a bubble about 6 cm long. This is going to be the dog's nose.

3. Now twist the balloon again to make two more bubbles next to your first one. These are going to be the dog's ears and should be about 3 cm long.

4. Bend back the dog's nose bubble against the balloon. Now twist the first and last twists together four or five times to make a supertwist. This will stay together and make the dog's head.

5. Make another twist about 6 cm along the balloon. This bubble will make the dog's neck.

6. Now it's time to make the legs. Hold on to the dog's neck and then twist another 6 cm bubble. Keeping hold of this first bubble, twist another bubble the same size. Now twist the two legs together with a supertwist.

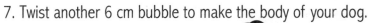

7. Twist another 6 cm bubble to make the body of your dog.

8. Then make another pair of legs in the same way as you did the first and join these together with a supertwist. Your sausage dog is now ready to hand out to the birthday boy or girl.

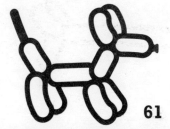

Make it magic

A magic show can be a great way to wow a children's party. First you'll need to learn some magic tricks. Get a book out of the library to help you or invest in a box of magic tricks.

A great magician needs the right name. You could be the Amazing Alexander or the Mysterious Madeleine — choose a name that has a magical ring. This will impress any parents who want to book you.

Practise your tricks to perfect your magic show. At your party performance, get the kids involved. Every magician needs an assistant. Be confident and if a trick goes wrong, quickly move on to the next one. Build up to a big finale that will amaze your audience.

Party puppets

Team up with a friend to put on a puppet show. Start off by writing a script for your show — you could include the names of party guests and the birthday boy and girl to give this the personal touch.

Practise making your puppets move. Put on different voices for the different characters. You could buy a ready-made puppet theatre with hand puppets or use a cardboard box to build your own stage set with sock puppet stars.

How to make a sock puppet

You will need:

- Some old socks
- A packet of googly eyes (you can buy these from a craft shop)
- Different coloured pieces of felt
- A felt-tip pen
- A pair of scissors
- PVA glue

1. Pick up one of your old socks and slide your hand inside. Use your fingers and thumb to make a mouth for your puppet.

2. Dot the felt-tip pen to mark where the eyes go. Then stick on the googly eyes.

3. Cut out felt shapes to decorate your sock puppet. You could create dragon scales or a snake's tongue.

4. Stick on the felt using PVA glue to finish your puppet.

Showtime! Set up a curtain behind the puppets' stage and hide behind it when you put on the show. Try to move the puppets in a realistic way. Don't forget to take a bow at the end.

How to house-sit

If your neighbours are going on holiday they might need somebody to look after their house. By popping in before and after school to make sure their home is still in one piece, you could earn yourself a treat when they get back.

Before they go away, get a list of the jobs they want you to do. These might be:

• Watering their plants. It's best to do this in the morning.

• Taking in their post. Don't leave letters hanging out of the letter box as this might tell burglars that the owners are away.

• Keeping an eye on the house. If you spot anyone suspicious hanging around, call the police.

Lock up the house each time you leave and don't leave any windows open. Looking after somebody's home is a very responsible job. Don't throw any parties while they're away!

How to sweep snow for dough

When the weather turns chilly, this gives you the chance to make a cool profit. If your road gets snowed in, you could be quids in. Get yourself a spade and knock on your neighbours' doors to ask if they'd like their driveways cleared. Offer a fair price to sweep the snow from their path. If you invest in some rock salt, you could charge extra to grit the drive to keep the path clear.

Defrosting car windscreens can be another money-earner. Get yourself some de-icing spray and turn that frost into dust! If the cold weather continues, recruit your friends to help. The more of you there are to clear the snow, the more money you'll all make!

SALT

USE YOUR HEAD

Get ready to give your brainpower a boost with some smart ways to make some extra cash.

This section will tell you how to:

- Get quick cash as a quiz show champ
- Win competitions and make a million in prizes
- Flog your story to a magazine
- Add to your pocket money by selling your opinions
- Use your brainpower as a homework helper
- Create an invention that will make you a fortune

It's time to put on your thinking cap and make some cash!

How to become a quiz show champ

If you're really brainy, why not take part in a TV quiz show? There are loads of shows on the lookout for clever young contestants. Check out the websites for different TV channels and quizzes to find out how to take part.

Before you get picked to appear on TV, you'll need to pass an audition. This might mean taking part in a practice quiz, so keep calm and make sure you're first on the buzzer. If you don't make it onto the TV, don't worry — some quizzes let you play along at home and you can phone in for the chance to win a prize. Karen Shand won £1 million by phoning into the TV quiz show The Vault. Be careful though, these calls can cost a fortune too, so make sure you get permission to call from your parents first.

How to win competitions

Fancy a mountain of cash, a brand-new bike or a fantastic holiday for all your friends and family? You can win all these things and more just by entering a competition.

You can find competitions everywhere: on websites, in magazines and newspapers, even on the side of your cereal box! There are thousands of competitions to enter and if you were lucky enough

to win them all, you would be a multi-millionaire! There are lots of different ways to win a competition:

- Some competitions just ask you to fill in your personal details.

Warning – make sure the competition isn't a scam before you fill in your details. To stop yourself getting a ton of spam, set up a special email address that you just use to enter competitions.

- Survey competitions ask you to complete a questionnaire. Answer the questions and you'll be entered into a prize draw.
- Some competitions ask you to come up with a catchy slogan for the product offering the prize. Use a rhyming dictionary to help you to think up a winning slogan.
- Some competitions will get you to show off your skills. This might mean writing a short story or taking a great picture. If the judges like your entry the best, you'll scoop the prize.

Be careful of competitions that ask you to call a number to collect your prize. Most of the time the number costs a fortune to phone and you the prize is worth less than the cost of the call!

Remember to follow the rules of the competition. Check you're old enough to enter and make sure you don't miss the closing date. The more competitions you enter, the more chances you have of winning. Good luck!

How to sell your story

Looking for a way to make some quick cash? It could be as easy as writing a letter to your favourite magazine. Lots of magazines offer money and prizes for the letters they print, so if your letter is picked you could be quids in.

First of all, take a trip to your local newsagent and flick through the magazines on the shelves. Find the letters pages and check out the money and prizes on offer. Some magazines only give a prize to one star letter every month, but others give out prizes for every letter that's printed.

Pick the magazines that give the prizes you want to win — this could be £50 for a star letter in *Bella* magazine or new science-fiction books from *SFX* magazine. Read through the letters to work out what kind of letters they like to print. These might be:

• Funny stories — some magazine like their readers to share funny things that have happened to them. Think about what funny stories you could share about your life.

• Real-life experiences — the letters you write could be serious too. If the magazine has recently featured an article about something you know about, maybe a problem you've experienced like bullying, you could write a letter about this.

• Views and opinions — maybe you've read something in the magazine that you want to rave or rant about. Magazines love to print letters that say nice things about them!

• Advice and tips — some magazines like to include handy hints that will help their readers. This could be tips about keeping fit, advice on how to get back with your boyfriend, or even making your own jam.

Now get your pen and paper and start writing your letter. Lots of magazines will let you email your letter, so you won't even have to waste money on a stamp. Now you've just got to wait for the next issue of the magazine to see if your letter is picked and then start counting the pennies.

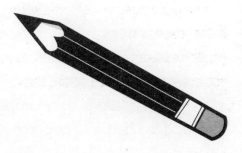

How to sell your opinions

Do you like to tell people what you think? Market research companies will pay to hear your opinions!

Questionnaires and surveys

Companies who make toys, fashion accessories and fast food snacks need to find out what young people think. This helps them make popular new products and work out better ways to sell you stuff.

To give your opinions, you can fill in surveys online. You'll find these surveys at market research websites aimed at young people like Dubit and MySurvey. These websites will reward you with cash, high street vouchers, free cinema tickets and music downloads for filling in each survey. First of all, you need to get your parents' permission and check that you're old enough to join the site.

You can also find questionnaires in newspapers and magazines. Some of these offer prizes to encourage you to complete them. You could find you've won a £1,000 just by answering a few questions!

Be a trendsetter

As well as asking your opinion, some companies want you to test out their products and show them off to your friends. By becoming a "brand ambassador" you can make money and get free gifts by:

- Giving feedback on a new product

- Setting up events and parties where you show off the new product to your school friends
- Sending emails and instant messages where you chat about the product
- Posting positive reviews on message boards and social networks

Being a super-fan for the brand can get you some great rewards, but make sure you don't let your friends down by giving a great review to something you don't like.

How to make your brain work for you

Are you smarter than your teacher? Do your friends ask for your help whenever a tricky test looms? Here's how you can turn your brainpower into earning power.

Homework helper

Become a homework helper. This doesn't mean you do your friends' homework for them – but you could help other students with subjects they're struggling with. So if you're an ace at English or a maths magician, you could help with puzzling punctuation or fiendish fractions.

Set a price for your services. This might be £1 for each homework help session. Remember to make the help you give fun – you don't want to turn into a boring teacher!

How to invent a fortune

Is your mind always buzzing with ideas and inventions? Can you think of solutions to problems that nobody else can solve? If that's the case, then you might be in with a chance of inventing your way to billion-pound bank account.

Eureka!

Don't think you have to be a grown-up to come up with a great invention. Did you know that the calculator, the helicopter, and even the trampoline were all invented by teenagers?

So, what's the secret to thinking up a great invention? Follow these steps to find out how:

$(z+2i)$ $(z+2i)(z+2)(z+2i)(z+2i)(z+2i)(z+2i)(z+2i)(z+2i)$
$(z+2i)$ $(z+2i)(z+2)(z+2i)(z+2i)(z+2i)(z+2i)=(z+2)$

Step 1 – Find a problem to solve

The best inventions solve problems. These don't have to be big problems, but can just be the little irritating things that make life suck. When Stephen Perry kept on losing important papers back in the 1840s, he decided to make something that would hold them together and invented the rubber band.

Step 2 – Put your brain in overdrive

Once you've found the problem you want to solve, get brainstorming. Try to come up with as many ideas to solve the problem as you can. Don't worry about coming up with silly ideas as some of the best inventions have started this way.

For each idea that you have, draw what the invention would look like. You could sketch this out on paper or use a computer to create the design of your invention. Label your drawing to show the invention's different features and how these would work. You might not come up with the perfect invention first time, but keep on trying!

Step 3 – See if it works

You've had your great idea, but will it really work? The only way to find out is to build a prototype of your invention. A prototype is a model of your invention that actually works.

When teenager Peter Ash was looking for a new way to charge his mobile phone, he decided to invent the Hamster-Charger! To build his prototype Peter hooked up a system of gears and a generator to his hamster Elvis's exercise wheel. Every time Elvis went for a spin, he charged up Peter's phone at the same time!

Step 4 – Protect your bright idea

To stop anyone copying your invention, you need to patent it. You can apply for a patent online from the Intellectual Property Office. Check out their website to find out what they need to know. If you get a patent, it means that you are the only person who is allowed to make and sell your invention.

Don't forget to check that nobody else has had the same idea and patented the invention before you. If they have, you'll have to head back to the drawing board.

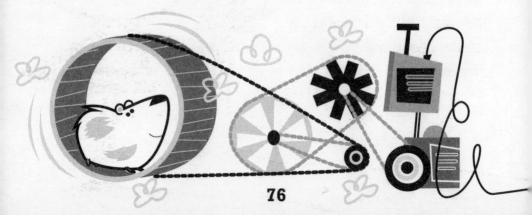

Step 5 – Sell your invention to the world

Now it's time to bring your invention out of the shed and into the shops. You'll need to:

- Think of a catchy name for your invention.
- Make lots of your invention so you've got stock to sell.
- Persuade shops to put your invention on their shelves.
- Advertise so that everyone knows about your great new invention and what it does. You could post a video on YouTube of your invention in action to create a buzz about it or get tweeting and blogging to take your message to the world.

All this will cost a lot of cash, so you might have to team up with a rich businessman or company who will invest in your invention. You'll have to share the profits, but they can help you make your invention a success. Good luck!

MAKE MONEY, SAVE THE WORLD

Is saving the environment just as important to you as saving some cash? If you're looking for some ways to make money that will make the world a better place as well, check out the ideas on the following pages.

This section will tell you how to:

- Recycle your rubbish to get rich quick
- Get rid of your clutter for cash
- Get gardening to make your money grow
- Raise cash for charity with fun fundraising ideas

Now let's get ready to turn trash into cash!

How to raise money for good causes

If you want to put your money-making skills to good use, why don't you try and raise some cash for charity instead of keeping all the money yourself? Here are some great ideas to get you started.

• Take a challenge — climbing a mountain, running a marathon, swimming the English Channel — there are lots of challenges you could take. Get your friends and family to sponsor you for every metre you climb, every mile you run or every length that you swim. Don't forget to train to make sure you make as much money as you can.

• Break a record — becoming a record breaker can be a fun way to fundraise. Footie fan Paul Newton raised thousands of pounds for charity by organizing a five-a-side football match that lasted for 40 hours! Try to think up some crazy records you could break.

• Organize an event — raffles, book sales, cake bake-offs, fundraising auctions — think about what sort of event would raise the most money where you live. If you can get publicity for your event in the local paper, you'll attract more people and make more cash.

• Use your skills — are you a great dancer, a talented artist or maybe a fantastic cook? Think of ways you could use your talents to raise cash. How about a sponsored dance-a-thon, painting portraits of people for money or baking biscuits and cakes to sell?

How to turn rubbish into cash

If you want to save the environment at the same time as making some cash, then get ready to recycle. Here are three great ways to turn yesterday's rubbish into money for tomorrow's treats.

Can cashback

Do you know that nearly seven billion cans of drink are guzzled in Great Britain every year? All these aluminium cans can be recycled to make new cans. If you can collect enough cans to recycle you could earn yourself some extra pocket money.

Contact your local recycling centre to check if they pay for aluminium cans. If they don't, you can find special recycling centres that will by looking at the website Thinkcans.com. This will show you where your nearest can recycling centre is. These special centres only pay out for every kilo of cans they receive – that's about 70 cans – so you'll need to get collecting first.

Make sure any aluminium cans don't get thrown into the bin at home. Tell your parents, brothers and sisters to save their cans and set up a special box in the kitchen to collect them. Crush the cans first to save space and make room for more. You could also offer to tidy the litter around your school or local youth club. Keep any cans that you find to one side to add to your recycling haul.

Remember, not all cans are made from aluminium, so you'll need to test them first. Look out for the symbol 'alu' which tells you that the can is aluminium. If you can't spot this, use a magnet instead. If it doesn't stick, then the can can be recycled!

Money for old mobiles

If you've got an old mobile phone that you don't use any more, don't throw it away. You might be able to sell your old phone for a tidy profit.

Check online to find companies that will buy your old phone such as mopay.co.uk. Use a website that compares the prices that different companies will pay for your phone. All you have to do is type in the make and model of your phone to find the best deal. If the price is right, then they'll send you a prepaid envelope to pop your phone in the post back to them. Once they've got your phone, you'll get the cash.

Don't worry if your phone doesn't work any more. Some companies will still buy faulty phones and try to fix these themselves.

How to sell your clutter

Take a look around your bedroom. What can you see? Chances are there are loads of DVDs that you've watched, books you've read and video games you've played, but won't ever look at again. Here's how to sell these to clear some space for new purchases.

Get selling online

There are lots of websites where you can sell unwanted CDs, DVDs, video games and books. The trick is to find the one where you'll make the most cash.

• The Musicmagpie website will tell you in a second how much money it will give you for your gear. All you have to do is scan or key in the barcode on the back of your CD, game or DVD and you'll instantly be offered a price for it. If you want to sell, just print off a label to post this off for free and wait for your cheque to arrive.

• You can sell your old books at online bookshops like Amazon. Search the website for the book you want to sell. On the page about the book, click on the "Sell yours here" button. You'll have to enter info about the book you're selling. Be honest if it's got a creased cover and a few dog-eared pages. Look at the prices other people are charging for the book before setting your own. You'll have more chance of selling yours if it's the cheapest on the site.

• You can also sell your stuff on auction websites like eBay. This site lets buyers bid what they want to pay on whatever you're selling. At the end of the auction, the person with the highest bid wins. You need to be 18 or over to sell things on eBay, so get a grown-up to sell your stuff for you. Give the item you're selling an appealing description and post up a photo of it too.

Car boot seller

If you've got a ton of clutter you want to get rid of in one go, pester your parents into helping you sell it at a car boot sale. These are great places to get rid of your booty — check online to find the nearest one to you. You'll have to pay a fee to set up your pitch, but this can be a great investment.

Get to the car boot sale early to set up your stuff. Lots of bargain-hunters will be there and you want to make sure that they see what you've got for sale. Price things up at 25% more than you want to sell them for — this gives you room to negotiate. The person buying will feel like they're getting a bargain, but you'll get the price you want. Make everything half-price at the end of the day to get rid of your stuff. Hopefully, you should make a tidy profit.

How to turn your green fingers into gold

If you've got green fingers and can tell the difference between a weed and a wild flower, why not set up your own gardening business? Lots of people will pay you money to keep their gardens looking neat and tidy.

Getting started

Think about who might be interested in your gardening business: busy people who don't have time to do the weeding, elderly people who might not be able to mow their lawn any more. Target your market to maximize your chances of getting gardening jobs. Ask if you can put up an advert at your local doctor's surgery – people who are poorly won't feel up to doing the gardening!

Make fliers advertising your services. These should have details of the different jobs you will do: weeding, watering plants and shrubs, mowing lawns, raking leaves, pruning, planting and fruit picking. If it's in the garden, you should be able to keep it looking good. Advertise your prices and make sure new customers know how to get in touch with you.

Gardening gear

A good gardener needs the right kit. Some of your customers might

let you use their lawnmower, but you'll look more professional if you've got your own gear. Here's a list of your must-have tools and what you should use them for.

- A spade – great for digging things
- A trowel – perfect for getting rid of weeds
- A rake – helps clear leaves and clippings
- A watering can – ideal for potted plants
- Gardening gloves – to stop your hands

from getting scratched and keep them clean!

You might need a few extra tools depending on the jobs. Be careful – if you're pruning plants you'll need secateurs or garden shears and these are sharp! Remember to get permission from your parents before you use any garden tools. If you want save time, a hosepipe lets you water lots of plants quickly.

Get gardening

Once you've got your first customer, make sure you do a good job. If you're mowing their lawn, don't miss any corners and always tidy up after yourself. The best advert for your business is their garden looking great. Friends and neighbours will see the results and might become your next customers.

Depending on the time of year, you'll need to do different tasks to keep a garden tidy.

- Spring – sowing seeds, planting shrubs, mowing lawns, pruning plants, tidying borders
- Summer – watering plants, trimming hedges, taking cuttings, mowing lawns
- Autumn – clearing leaves, tidying shrubs, mowing lawns, planting bulbs for next year
- Winter – brushing paths, scrubbing patios, covering potted plants to protect them from frost

As well as their gardens, some people keep allotments where they grow fruit and vegetables. Leaflet your local allotments with your fliers to see if anybody needs any help. You could offer to look after people's allotments when they go away on holiday. Instead of getting paid in cash, you could ask to be paid in fruit and veg which you can then sell yourself!

You can also make a profit by growing your own plants and vegetables. Here's how to get started.

How to grow a plant from a cutting

If you've got lots of plants growing in your garden, you could take cuttings from these to try and grow some new plants to sell.

You will need:

- A medium-sized plant pot
- Secateurs or garden shears (be careful – these are sharp!)
- Compost
- A spray mister
- A clear plastic bag
- An elastic band

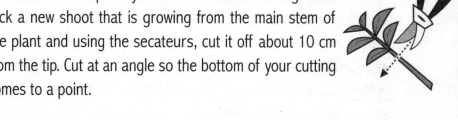

1. Choose the plant you want to take a cutting from. Pick a new shoot that is growing from the main stem of the plant and using the secateurs, cut it off about 10 cm from the tip. Cut at an angle so the bottom of your cutting comes to a point.

Warning – ask an adult to help you do this.

2. Remove any leaves from near the bottom of the shoot. Now your cutting is ready to plant. You could take more cuttings from the same plant, but don't take too many or else the plant might die!

3. Fill your plant pot with compost. Pat this down firmly, leaving about a centimetre of space at the top of the pot.

4. Insert your cuttings into the plant pot. It's best to space these out around the edge of the pot to give them room to grow. Don't forget to water the cuttings.

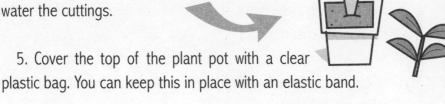

5. Cover the top of the plant pot with a clear plastic bag. You can keep this in place with an elastic band.

6. Keep your plant pot out of direct sunlight and water with the spray mister occasionally to keep the cuttings moist.

7. After eight weeks, you can transplant each of the cuttings that have grown into their own plant pot. Be careful when you do this to make sure you don't damage the new roots. Your potted plants are now ready to sell!

Not all plants will grow from cuttings, but herbs like rosemary, sage and thyme are great ones to try.

Make your sales bloom

If you have a school fair, you could set up a stall and sell your plants there — or you could sell them from your front gate! Make a sign to show what you're selling. Remember to include the names and prices of your plants on the sign.

How to grow your own vegetables

Crunchy carrots

1. Get a large plant pot at least 30 cm deep and fill this with potting compost.

2. Sprinkle some carrot seeds over the top and cover with more compost.

3. Keep the carrots watered as they grow. You'll need to wait two to three months until they're fully grown before you can pull up your carrot crop.

Tasty tomatoes

You can grow tomatoes from seeds – a great type to choose is the tumbler tomato, which you can grow in a tub.

1. Start off by sowing the tomato seeds in a seed tray. Sprinkle them on the surface and then cover with more compost.

2. Keep the seed tray in a warm, sunny place like a windowsill above a radiator. Cover the tray with a clear plastic lid and spray the soil with water to help the seeds grow.

3. When the seedlings are about 6 cm tall, transplant them into a pot. Put the pot in a sunny place and water every day.

4. Feed the tomatoes with fertilizer to encourage them to grow. Get a grown-up to help you, and follow the instructions carefully.

5. Wait 2–3 months for the tomatoes to ripen. Then they'll be ready to pick.

Perfect potatoes

You can grow great-tasting spuds in an old dustbin!

1. Make some holes in the bottom of the bin to let water drain out and then fill it up with compost.

2. Get some seed potatoes from your local garden centre and put four or five of these on top with their sprouts pointing up.

3. Cover the seed potatoes with another layer of compost and keep watering them well.

4. Keep your bin in a bright part of the garden so the potato leaves get enough sun. In a few months' time you'll have a crop of perfect potatoes.

WORK YOUR WAY TO WEALTH

If you're not scared of some hard work, you can use the ideas on the following pages to earn yourself some hard cash.

This section will tell you how to:

- Clean houses, cars and windows to earn extra cash
- Bag a bargain as a personal shopper
- Make a profit by taking care of pets
- Deliver newspapers to boost your income
- Organize your parents' lives as a top PA

Now get ready — it's time to clean up cash-wise!

How to clean up cash-wise

If you're willing to get your hands dirty, you could make some cash by setting up your own cleaning business. Here are three money-spinning ideas.

Car cleaning

Do you know how much it costs to take a car to the car wash? If you could undercut these prices and still make a profit, you could have a booming business.

To clean a car you'll need the following equipment:

- A sponge
- A cloth
- A scrubbing brush
- Car shampoo
- Car wax
- A bucket
- Lots of water

Make fliers advertising your car washing business and hand them out to your family and friends. You could offer a range of prices for a simple polish to a full valet service where you clean the car inside and out. Start off with an introductory offer – a half-price car wash – to drum up some business. If you do a good job, customers will ask you to clean their car every week.

Don't just wait for customers to come to you. Go along to events like school fetes where there are lots of people. Ask your teacher if you could set up a car cleaning space in the car park and split the profits with the school. Be polite when you approach potential customers to ask them if they want their car washed and remember to stay safe. Make sure an adult is with you at all times and stay away from any moving cars.

Window-cleaner

Look out of your window. Does it look grubby? With a squeegee, a bucket and some washing-up liquid you could soon put that right.

Start by asking your parents if you can clean the windows of your house. You might earn extra pocket money, but more importantly it will let your practise your window-cleaning skills.

Warning – only clean the inside of the windows when you move upstairs. You don't want to fall out!

When you can clean a window in less than a minute, it's time to make your business professional.

Visit shops in your local area. Lots of these will have large windows at the front that soon get grubby.

Ask if you could clean their windows every week to keep their business looking good. Remember to make some fliers to advertise your window-cleaning service. You could ask satisfied customers to pass these fliers on to their friends.

House-cleaner

Some families with busy lives employ cleaners to get jobs done around the house. If you're a whiz with the hoover and can dust a room in five minutes flat, why don't you clean up by offering your services?

Ask around your family to see if anybody needs a cleaner. You'll have to be willing to do the jobs that your customers don't want to do – cleaning toilets, scrubbing floors and catching all the cobwebs. Don't start complaining if you chip a nail or a spider falls in your hair. The money you get will make up for it!

How to become a personal shopper

If you love shopping and are great at bagging a bargain, why not become a personal shopper? This is a great opportunity to turn your money-spending ways into a money-making scheme. A personal shopper is somebody who buys things for busy people who don't have the time to shop themselves.

What do you need to be a personal shopper?

A personal shopper must be:

• Trustworthy – if you're spending someone's shopping budget they'll want to know you'll spend it wisely. Whether it's the weekly food shop for your gran or finding a party dress for a busy fashionista, keep your receipts to prove what you've spent.

• A bargain-hunter – if someone's paying you to do their shopping, you'll need to prove you're worth it by saving them money. Compare prices and look out for offers. Looking online can help you bag the biggest savings.

• Stylish – personal shoppers who specialize

in fashion need to have a great sense of style. As well as keeping up with the latest trends, you need to know what type of clothes would suit the person you're shopping for. Take a look through their wardrobe before you get started.

You could start by offering a free personal shopper experience to your family and friends. If you get the shopping they want and save them some money too – they might pay you next time.

How to make pots of money out of pets

The pet industry is worth billions of pounds. People who love animals love to spend money on them too, so this is the perfect business opportunity. Here are three great ideas to help you make a pet profit.

Pet-sitter

If your neighbours are going on holiday but have to leave their pet behind, offer to pet-sit for them. Before they leave, find out:

• What the pet eats and how often it needs to be fed. If there's more than one pet to take care of, make sure you don't mix up their meals. It's tricky getting Pedigree Chum out of a fish tank!

• If they need to be exercised. Dogs will need walking, but you won't have much luck getting a lead on a guinea pig.

• How often you need to clean out their cage/basket/tank — delete as applicable!

Keep a close eye on the pet while you're looking after it – you don't want to end up with an escaped anaconda! Get a contact telephone number to call in case of emergencies.

Dog-walker

This is a great way to keep fit and make some money too, but you need to love dogs to take on this job. For a dog owner who's got a busy job, a broken leg or is just running out of puff, a professional dog walker can be the answer to their prayers.

Make fliers and print business cards to advertise your dog-walking service. You could give your business a catchy name like Pet Patrol to stand out from the crowd. Remember to include information about where you'll walk the dog and how much you'll charge.

Don't be tempted to take on too many clients. There's a limit to how many dogs you can fit on one lead. Remember you're supposed to be taking them for a walk not the other way round! Take a few doggie treats along on each walk and don't forget your poop scoop.

Pet pamperer

Lots of owners like to treat their pets, so why not set up a dog grooming service.

Warning – only groom a dog that you know well and ask an adult to supervise you. Some dogs don't like getting their hair washed and might turn nasty!

How to groom a dog

Follow these steps to get a mucky mutt looking like a prince. You will need:
- A dog brush
- Shampoo
- A non-slip bathmat
- A plastic collar
- A jug
- A towel

1. Put the non-slip mat in the bottom of the bath. Then get the dog in the bath. You might need a toy to tempt them. If the dog is difficult to control you could slip the plastic collar on – the dog not you!

2. Fill the jug with diluted shampoo. Wet the dog and start washing them from the back to the front. You want to leave the head for last.

3. Wash the dog's head and face. Be careful not to get shampoo in their eyes or water in their ears. Rinse the shampoo off and then towel the dog dry.

4. Use the brush to comb the dog's coat. Make sure you brush in the direction that the hair grows to keep the dog looking great. Brush out any knots of hair that you find under the legs and other hard to reach places.

How to deliver a profit

Fancy getting a bit of exercise while you earn some extra cash? Delivering newspapers can be great way to keep you and your bank account fit and healthy.

Paper round

If you don't mind getting up early, try to get a job as a paperboy or -girl. Ask your local newsagent if they need anyone to deliver their newspapers. If any jobs are available, find out how much each newsagent pays and how many papers they'll expect you to deliver. You'll want to choose the one that pays the most for the least amount of work! Remember though, you need to be thirteen or older to work as a paperboy or -girl.

When you've got the job, do your research. Work out the quickest route to deliver all the papers you have. You might want to take a street map with you for your first few deliveries to make sure you don't get lost. You could use a bike to get around more quickly. If you do this, make sure you've got the right lights on your bike and wear a high visibility jacket when mornings are dark.

Most paperboys and -girls work Monday to Saturday, but you can also get a job delivering the Sunday papers. Be careful — these are the heavy ones! Take a shopping trolley to help you carry all the extra sections and free magazines that the Sunday papers come with.

When you get your wages at the end of the week, make sure you don't spend them all on sweets from the newsagent.

How to be a top PA

Does your dad always forget things? Is your mum always in a muddle? If you've got great organizational skills, you could help organize their busy lives and earn some extra money as your parents' PA!

What is a PA?

A PA is a personal assistant. This is somebody who helps to organize the person they are helping.

What does a parents' PA do?

Anything that helps make your parents' lives less stressful! This might mean:

- Answering telephone calls and taking messages
- Reminding them about the things they have to do that day, e.g. don't forget to pick up the dry-cleaning
- Opening letters, sorting bills and throwing away the junk mail
- Organizing events, e.g. helping to book the family holiday
- Helping out with important chores, e.g. making a list of the groceries they need to buy and shopping for these on the internet
- Researching information, e.g. looking up reviews to help choose a new TV

If you can keep your parents' lives running smoothly, you'll be worth your weight in gold. Don't forget to agree your wage before you start – you don't want to end up doing lots of extra chores for free!

MAKE A TECHNO-TON

Fancy yourself as a digital whiz? If you want to turn your virtual dreams into money-making schemes, get connected with these cutting-edge ideas.

This section will tell you how to:

- Sell ringtones to make your bank account buzz
- Download some cash by creating your own apps
- Make money by writing a blog
- Set up an internet business to become a dotcom millionaire
- Get cash by giving gadget advice
- Make money by playing video games

Ring! Ring! Quick, turn the page — that could be the sound of a million pounds!

How to sell your own ringtones

Can you hear the sound of a mobile phone ringing? That could be the sound of money in your pocket. Selling ringtones for mobile phones is big business and can make you a crazy profit.

The billion-dollar frog

What do you think the biggest-selling ringtone of all time is? A chart-topping tune? A hot hip-hop track? It's actually the Crazy Frog – an annoying animated amphibian who makes motorcycle noises! More than 50 million people have downloaded the Crazy Frog ringtone. This has made hundreds of millions of pounds for the company who sells it!

Ringtone research

So, how can you come up with a cool ringtone that everyone will want to buy? Start off by checking out websites that sell ringtones and see what the best-sellers are. These might be:

- Hot new songs
- Video-game sounds
- Strange sound effects
- Football chants
- Funny voices and catchphrases

You might not be able to write a top-selling tune, but you could come up with some funny catchphrases.

Make the right call

You now need to record your ringtone. Hook up a microphone to your computer and use a free software package like Audacity to help you to do this. Remember you need to make your ringtone into a computer file that people can download.

• You could use some music software to help create a catchy ringtone. Remember you're not trying to write a pop song, just a 40-second tune that will grab someone's attention when their phone starts to ring.

• Look for things that could help you make your own sound effects. Record the sound of dog food sliding out of a tin can – this can sound like an alien tentacle coming to grab you! Try different things to find the sound effects you need for your ringtone.

• Get some friends round and record chants for your favourite football teams. These will be the perfect ringtone for any footie fan.

• Think about what makes your friends laugh. If you're good at impressions, you could make yourself sound like a famous celeb saying something silly!

Download your fortune

When you've got your ringtones, you need to find somewhere to sell them. Some ringtone websites will let you sell your own. You could also advertise your ringtones on MySpace and let people listen to samples before they buy. If enough people like your ringtones, you'll soon hear the jingle of money ringing in your ears!

How to create and sell your own apps

If you want to make some serious money, there's an app for that! An app is a little package of software that can help you do something. Whether it's helping you find a bargain, take control of your budget or keep an eye on the price of stocks and shares, there are tons of smartphone apps that you can download. However, the smart money can be made by creating and selling your own apps.

True story of a tech-tycoon

When American teenager, Robert Nay, decided to design his own app, he didn't realize it would end up topping the iTunes chart. Fourteen-year-old Robert had an idea for a fun new game – Bubble Ball – where players use tools and puzzle pieces to steer a ball around the screen.

Robert designed the different levels of his game and taught himself how to code the app from scratch using a book he had borrowed from the library. In less than a month, he had finished the game and uploaded it to both the Apple App Store and Android Marketplace.

After trying out this addictive new game, one website named Bubble Ball as their App of the Week and the game started to race up the charts. Only two weeks after it had first been released, Bubble Ball had been downloaded more than a million times. After two months, the game topped seven million downloads – it was a hit!

Although Bubble Ball was a free app, if Robert had charged a dollar for every download, it would have made him a multi-millionaire.

Making your own app

You don't have to be a whiz at computer programming to create your own app. Follow these steps to start getting appy!

Step 1 – Have a brilliant idea

There are hundreds of thousands of apps already out there. If your app is going to become a bestseller, it'll need to be special. Use your imagination to think of a new idea that would make a great app. This might be:

• An addictive game that people can't stop playing even when they're on the move. From cute cartoon birds to rampaging zombies, bestselling games apps can be weird, wonderful, but most of all lots of fun to play.

• An app that makes people's lives easier. There are apps to keep you fit, make you smart, help you take better photographs and even organize your life. Think about a problem people need help with and then invent the app that could solve it.

• An app that lets you get creative. From making music to creating cool cartoons, there are loads of apps out there that help people show off their talents. See if you can create an inspirational app.

• A funny app that makes people laugh. Sometimes the silliest apps can become bestsellers.

Step 2 – Do your research

You've got your great idea, but now you need to check out the competition. Are there any other apps that are similar to your idea? Take a look at these to see how they work.

Think about what you like about your favourite apps. If it's a game, how do you play it? What happens when you tap a character or slide your finger across the screen? Working these things out can help you to make sure that your own game app is easy to play. Don't just look at apps that are already bestsellers – look at rubbish apps, too. You can spot mistakes and avoid them in your own app.

Step 3 – Design and program your app

Don't worry if you're not a hotshot computer programmer, the first step to designing your app is to sketch it all out on paper!

Make a drawing for each screen of your app. Think about what you want it to look like and add notes explaining what the person using it needs to be able to do. When you've got your app planned out on paper, you can turn your attention to designing and programming it. Apps need to be programmed using special computer code. If you don't know how to do this, you could teach yourself coding like teen tycoon Robert Nay, or team up with someone who can. However, there are also special tools such as App Inventor that allow you to create your own apps without learning how to code.

How to make money from your blog

There are millions of blogs out there on the internet. Some of these are written by famous people where they write about their glamorous lives, but most blogs are just written by someone like you. Maybe you've even already got your own blog where you write about the things you like. But did you know you can also blog your way to some extra cash?

Getting started

Before you set up your blog, you need to decide what you want to blog about. It's best to write about something you love. Here are some topics that other young bloggers have blogged about:

• Food – are you a budding Jamie Oliver? Why not set up a blog where you share your favourite recipes like teenage chef Sam Stern? Give people your top cooking tips and share any culinary disasters you've had, too.

• Fiction – always got your head in a book? Start a blog where you review the books you read. That's what a ten-year-old girl in the United States did and now her blog Laura's Life is read by lots of famous authors and publishers send her books for free!

• Fashion – like to look good and stay in style? Keep up to date with the latest fashion trends? Take a leaf out of teen blogger Tavi's book. Her fashion blog Style Rookie gets 50,000 hits a day. Designers give her free clothes, and she's invited to fashion shows all over the world!

True story of a fashion blog tycoon

Poppy Dinsey made a New Year's resolution to keep an online fashion diary every day for a year. She'd show off a different outfit every day and talk about her style likes and dislikes.

Poppy's fashion followers now go to her site to check out her outfits and get fashion tips — but Poppy is turning her style sense into a business as well. A mobile phone company sponsored Poppy to be their official blogger at London fashion week. Poppy also plans to turn her website into a social network, which would make money from advertising and links to fashion brands.

Build your blog

You can use free software to get your blog started. Blogger and Wordpress are two websites that can help you set up your blog for free. Choose a name for your blog that tells people what you'll be writing about. If you're going to be reviewing video games, you don't want to call your blog My Favourite Fluffy Kittens! Pick a name that will help your blog stand out from the crowd.

Get blogging

It's time to start typing and get people reading your blog. Remember, there are millions of blogs out there, but if you can make your blog funny, friendly and informative, people will want to read yours.

Make some money

Here are a few ways you can start earning cash from your blog:

• Advertising. Free computer programs like Google AdSense help you put adverts on your blog. If someone clicks on the ad, you get paid a few pence. The more clicks you get, the more cash you earn!

• Selling. If you review a blockbuster movie, send your readers to buy the DVD by posting a link to an online store. Join Amazon Associates to get a slice of money from these sales.

• Freebies. The more readers your blog gets, the more chance you have of getting stuff for free. Books, gadgets, fashion accessories – if you review it, you could get sent new ones to try. Be honest – don't give something a great review just because you got it for free!

How to become a dotcom millionaire

Got a great idea about how to make money on the internet? Think you could set up a website that will be bigger than Amazon, Bebo and Facebook? On the internet you can reach millions of people all around the world. If you've got the right business idea, you could turn all these people into pound signs and become a dotcom millionaire.

Getting started

First of all you need a name for your website. Use an online service like 123-reg to check that the name you've chosen is available. If it is, you might be able to buy it for just a few pounds.

Once you've got your name, you need to build your website. You could buy some software such as Mr Site to help you build your own website, but it might be cheaper to team up with a friend who's good at web design.

Dotcom tips for success

A successful internet business might:

• Sell things – on the internet you can reach lots more customers that you ever could in an everyday shop. To succeed you need to provide your customers with a great service that they won't be able to find anywhere else. Amazon started as just another internet bookseller, but the way it made shopping for books so easy with reviews and recommendations soon made it the number one shopping site on the web. Now you can buy everything from clothes to computers from Amazon, making the business billions of pounds.

• Let people do something they want to but couldn't before – an internet business can use technology in exciting ways to bring customers to its website. Before YouTube started there wasn't one website where you could upload, share and watch videos. Now YouTube is one of the most popular sites in the world and the business was sold in 2006 for more than a billion dollars.

• Have a lot of users – the social networking site Facebook started off as a way for students in one American college to stay in touch. It now has more than 600 million users around the world and is valued at nearly £50 billion!

True stories of dotcom tycoons

Don't let your age stop you from starting up your own dotcom company. It didn't stop these two dotcom millionaires:

• Ashley Qualls set up her website whateverlife.com when she was just fourteen years old. A budding web designer she created the site to show off her design skills, but soon built up a huge audience of teenagers who wanted to download her graphics and layouts for their own websites and MySpace pages. As her website grew she turned down an offer of $1.5 million to sell whateverlife.com, but has now made more than a $1 million from the site herself!

• Alex Tew was a student when he set up his Million Dollar Homepage. This webpage is made up of a million tiny pixels which Alex sold to advertisers for a dollar a pixel. This crazy idea ended up netting Alex over a million dollars.

Don't become a dotcom disaster!

If you get the right idea and it looks like your internet business might be a big success, remember to keep your feet on the ground. Things can change quickly on the internet and today's hot new website can soon become yesterday's news.

The fashion website Boo.com spent tons of cash on snazzy graphics, TV adverts and 5-star hotels before they even launched the site. Boo.com's owners even hired a top hairdresser to create a hairstyle for a computer-generated character! This dotcom disaster spent £150 million in just over a year before going bust. Make sure you don't waste money on silly things.

How to make money playing games

What's your dream job? How does getting paid for playing video games sound? Here's how you can score plenty of pounds as well as points and make it to the top of the money-making leader board.

Video game tester

Fancy playing the hottest new video games before they're released? You need to get a job as a video-game tester. Most of these jobs are for adults as you have to work full-time at a video-game company testing the games. However, if you fancy giving it a try, why don't you see if there's a video-game company near you and contact them to ask if you can do some work experience in your school holidays. It might be your first step to becoming a top video-game designer.

For online games and mobile apps, some companies look for people to test these over the internet. This could be a way you could become a video-game tester without ever leaving the comfort of your chair! All you'll need to do is play the games and report any bugs that you find. You'll need to check that you're old enough to test the game and get your parents' permission first though.

Games reviewer

Do you tell all your friends when you find a great new video game or warn them about a real stinker? If you like giving your opinions about games, why not become a video-game reviewer?

There are thousands of video games released every year. Gamers need help to find the ones that are worth buying and they check out magazines, websites and blogs that rate the new releases.

To make a start as a video-game reviewer, you could contact these magazines and website to see if they're looking for any new reviewers. You'll need to show you can write, so send them some examples of your reviews. Look at the way they set their reviews out and make sure you follow this format. Try to make your review as fun and interesting to read as the game was to play. Actually, even if the game was rubbish you still need to write an interesting review!

Hints, tips and cheats

Are you always the first of your friends to finish a new video game? Why not write a walkthrough to help any gamers who get stuck and can't finish the game.

A walkthrough is a step-by-step guide that tells you how to win. It can give you hints and tips about how to get past traps, find hidden weapons and complete secret missions.

You could set up a blog where you post up your walkthroughs. If you get lots of readers you'll soon start to make money from your blog. Check out page 113 to find out more.

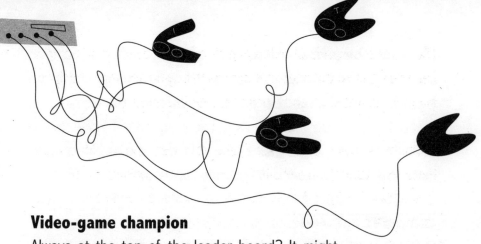

Video-game champion

Always at the top of the leader board? It might be time to turn your gaming skills into dollar bills. Video-game tournaments, where you compete with the best gamers from around the world, can reward the winners with big prizes, from 3D TVs to £100,000 prizes. Here are some top tips from a video-game champion:

• Play the games you love – to win a video-game tournament you'll have to play the same game over and over again. Choose a video game that you won't get bored of.

• Practise, practise, practise – to be the best you need to practise. Sharpen your skills by competing with friends and pick up tips about how to improve your score.

• Keep your cool – to win a tournament you'll need to be able to handle the pressure. Keep calm when you're playing the game and concentrate on winning.

Why don't you start by setting up your own video-game tournament? Turn to page 35 to find out how.

How to become a gadget guru

Do your parents always ask you for help when they crash the computer? Are you the only one who knows how the digital video recorder works? Do your friends ask your advice to help them find the hottest new apps for their phones? Find out how to make some extra cash by charging for your techno know-how.

Call the IT helpdesk

Problem with your broadband? Computer on the blink? Do you know that some IT helpdesks charge a £1 for every minute you're on the phone?

If you know how to sort out any PC problems or can get a laptop back in tip-top condition, why not set up your own IT helpdesk? Advertise your services to friends and family. Instead of charging your customers by the minute, how about asking for a treat for every problem you solve!

Computer care

You could also make some extra cash by helping people keep their computers safe from viruses and hacking attacks. Download and install the latest anti-virus software. You can often find this software for free online.

Gadget rundown

Here are some more ideas about how to make
money by giving gadget advice:

Mobile phones

Help your friends stay up to date with the latest apps. Create a list
of the top ten new apps you find every week. Recommend different
apps for the different things your friends like to do. Lots of apps
are free, so you can help them to save money as well as making
some yourself.

Digital cameras

Know someone who loves to take photos, but can't get their
camera to work properly? Why don't you run some digital camera
training to help them take great pictures? Show them what the
camera's different features do and give tips on how to improve
their camera skills.

The next big thing

There are loads of new gadgets coming out all the time — from robot massagers to 3D video-glasses. But how can you tell which gadget is going to be a great buy? If you know someone who is thinking of investing their cash in a hot new gadget, use your know-how to help them make the right choice. You could even charge for your services in helping them find the hottest new gear.

Stay up to date by reading reviews of the latest gadgets online to find out their good and bad points. You could go along to a shop to try out the gadget yourself. Ask the salesperson the right questions to find out if the gadget lives up to its hype.

You could even set up a blog where you post your gadget reviews and recommendations and make money at the same time. Check out page 113 to find out how.

FAME AND FORTUNE

Looking for a glamorous way to make some money? Here are some cool and creative careers that can make you pots of cash.

This section will tell you how to:

- Spin yourself a tidy profit by becoming a DJ
- Make money as a model
- Become a film director with a blockbuster bank account
- Make it as a film star to give your finances top billing
- Turn your sporting skills into gold

Let's find out how to turn fame into fortune.

How to become a DJ

Do you love music? Can you spot a hit song before it tops the charts? If you know how to get a crowd on to their feet and into their dancing shoes, you could make it big as a superstar DJ. Follow these steps to find out how.

Step 1 – Get the right gear

You can't start DJing until you've got the right equipment. A set of turntables or CD decks can cost a lot of money, but you can DJ using just a computer or your mobile phone by downloading a DJ app that lets you mix tracks together.

A DJ also needs a large music collection. You might want to stick to the type of music you like, but the best DJs have eclectic tastes. Try to learn about different styles of music and build up your collection with the best tracks.

Step 2 – Mix it up

Whatever equipment and tunes you choose, you need to practise your DJ skills. Spend time in your bedroom perfecting your techniques before you hit the dance floor. You will need to learn how to:

- Beatmix — this is where you match the bass beats of two different songs so you that you can switch seamlessly between them.
- Scratch — scratching is where you move a record backwards and forwards with your hand to create a scratching sound that you mix in over the top of another record.
- Backspin — this is where you rewind a record to make it spin backwards. This makes a cool sound effect and lets you cue up a catchy part of a song.
- Juggle beats — beat juggling is where you cut from one sample to another to create a unique track. The samples might be drum beats, guitar solos, vocal hooks — any sounds that will get the crowd dancing. You can find tutorials on YouTube to help you master these techniques.

Step 3 – Find a gig

You're ready to go, but where can you spin some tunes? Here are some ideas to get your DJ career off the ground:

- Friends' birthday parties and family weddings often need a DJ
- Offer to DJ at your local youth club
- Ask a teacher if you can DJ at the school disco

125

To persuade people to let you DJ, make a mix CD to show off your skills. Enter DJ competitions to show how you can rock a crowd. If you win, you'll soon have people begging you to DJ at their party or club. Remember to agree the price you will charge to perform your DJ set.

If you want to become a radio DJ instead, contact your local radio station to see if you can get some work experience in your school holidays. Radio 1 DJ Chris Moyles started his DJ career on hospital radio when he was still at school. You could also broadcast your own radio show over the internet to get yourself known.

Step 4 – Spin the wheels of steel
Whenever you play a set, remember these three golden rules:

1. Choose the tracks you play to fit the event – you don't want to play a banging house track at your granny's birthday party!

2. Keep one eye on the dance floor. If you can read a crowd and play the tunes they love, you'll keep them dancing.

3. End your set with a mega-hit track – one that's guaranteed to get the room shaking.

If you follow these rules, you'll soon be on your way to being a superstar DJ!

How to become a model

If you've got the right look then you might be able to make it as a model. Top models can earn millions a year from advertisements, cover shoots and fashion shows. You won't become a supermodel straight away, but if you follow these steps you might soon see your face staring out from the pages of a magazine.

Don't worry if you've not got the right look — fashions change and what's a hot look one minute can soon change. Remember, some of the strangest-looking people have made it as models!

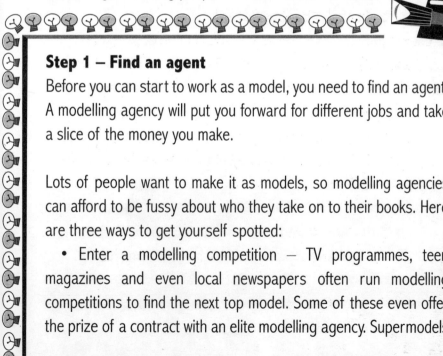

Step 1 – Find an agent

Before you can start to work as a model, you need to find an agent. A modelling agency will put you forward for different jobs and take a slice of the money you make.

Lots of people want to make it as models, so modelling agencies can afford to be fussy about who they take on to their books. Here are three ways to get yourself spotted:

• Enter a modelling competition — TV programmes, teen magazines and even local newspapers often run modelling competitions to find the next top model. Some of these even offer the prize of a contract with an elite modelling agency. Supermodels

Cindy Crawford and Gisele Bundchen both started out this way. Make sure you check how old you have to be to enter the competition and get your parents' permission first.

• Apply to a modelling agency – find out how to apply to a modelling agency by looking at their website. You might have to fill in an application form and they'll want to see a photo of you too. Ask a friend to take some headshots and full length portraits of you using a digital camera, and then choose the best ones to send. There are lots of agencies who work with younger models, but make sure you pick one with a good reputation. Don't forget to get your parents' permission before you apply.

• Get scouted – model agents are always on the lookout for fresh faces. They sometimes send scouts to big events like fashion exhibitions to try and spot potential models in the crowd. Top models like Kate Moss and Erin O'Connor were spotted this way.

Warning – be careful, some people pretend to be model scouts to scam wannabe models into paying them money. If you're approached by someone who says they're a model scout, take their business card and tell your parents.

Step 2 – Audition for a job

Once you've got an agent, you can start auditioning for modelling jobs. These might be for TV ads, photo shoots, or even music videos. You might want to be the next supermodel, but find yourself advertising dog food instead!

To increase your chances of getting picked at an audition, remember to be positive, punctual and polite. Don't worry if you get rejected – this just means that somebody else's face fitted instead. Even supermodels get rejected from time to time!

Step 3 – Strike a pose

Remember, life as a model isn't all glamour – it's a lot of hard work too. You should spend time practising posing and walking on a runway to make sure you're ready.

When you're in front of the camera, don't forget to follow the photographer's instructions. If you impress the client, you'll soon get more modelling jobs and make your bank account look good too!

How to become a film director

Want to make it big in Hollywood? Fancy earning mega-bucks as a director? All you need to get started is a video camera...

Make up a story

If you want people to watch the movies you make, you need to tell a good story. Watch your favourite films to see how they tell their stories. You could get inspiration for your film from books and TV programmes that you love, stories on the news or just events from everyday life. When you've made up your story, you need to...

Cast your film

Get your friends to audition for parts in the film. You won't have to pay them and as the director you'll get to boss them around too. Now you're ready to...

ACTION!

Get shooting

Break your story down into scenes. Think about where you could film each one. Maybe your back garden could be the location for a troll's den. Then grab your camera and start shooting. Tell your actors what you want them to do and shoot the same scene several times from different angles. This will come in handy when you...

Edit the film

Upload the footage you've filmed to a computer. Use a program like iMovie or Windows Movie Maker to edit your film — you'll be able to cut between scenes and add a soundtrack. Then you're ready to...

Premiere the movie

You could just show your film to your family and friends, but to make it as a big-name director you'll need a bigger audience. Enter your film into competitions, approach local film festivals to see if they'll show your movie and upload it to YouTube so the world can watch it.

That's what filmmaker Fede Alvarez did with his five-minute film Panic Attack. This mini-movie, which he made for a couple of hundred pounds, showed a fleet of robots and UFOs invading a city. In just a few weeks, his film got 1.5 million hits and a top Hollywood director called Fede up to offer him $30 million dollars to make a full-length science-fiction film. If your film hits the big time, Hollywood might be calling you next...

How to become a film star

Becoming a star of the silver screen can be a profitable career. Daniel Radcliffe was only ten years old when he auditioned for the first Harry Potter film and he's now a multi-millionaire. But you don't have to be a big star to make money from acting.

Start off small

First you need to learn how to act! Get involved in school plays, drama clubs and theatre groups. Practise learning your lines and don't be afraid to take on different parts — from the smallest to the biggest. Find out what kind of acting you enjoy the most. This might be comedy, drama, musicals, but don't just stick to one type. The more experience you get, the more you will improve your acting skills.

Find an agent

An agent will help you to find acting roles. They could get you a part as the star of a film or a job as an extra in a TV drama.

Use the internet to find a talent agent with a good reputation. Get your parents' permission before you get in touch with them. An agent will want to know how tall you are, what your age is, your acting experience and any hobbies and skills you have. Send them a photo too so they can see what you look like.

Get the part
Whether it's the starring role on a West End show or a part in a TV ad, you'll need to audition. Learn a speech or a scene from a film or play that you know to act out for the casting director. Try to be yourself and don't get nervous — you'll have a better chance of landing the part if you stay calm.

How to turn sporting skills into gold

Ever dreamt of walking out at Wembley and scoring a last-minute goal? Winning a medal at the Olympic Games? If you can make it as a sporting star, then you can turn your dreams into gold.

Soccer star
Top football clubs start signing up the stars of tomorrow from the age of seven. If you can show some fancy skills with a ball at your feet, you might have a chance of being scouted. Football scouts watch matches across the country to find any players with potential, so make sure you play for your local team.

Some big clubs also run summer schools to help you improve your soccer skills — David Beckham was first spotted by Manchester United at a summer soccer school when he was eleven years old. The former England captain is now said to be worth £125 million!

Crossbar challenge

You don't have to sign for a team to make big money from your sporting skills. Rugby fan Stuart Tinner had just gone along to watch the match on the day he won £250,000. Stuart was picked out of the crowd to take part in a half-time crossbar challenge. With a kick of the ball from the halfway line, he hit the crossbar and won a quarter of a million pounds! Time to start practising your kicking…

Olympic hero

Whatever sport you are good at — from sprinting to swimming, badminton to basketball, table tennis to the triathlon — you have the chance of stardom at the Olympic Games. Most Olympic athletes don't get paid, but if they make it into the medals they can get sponsored by big companies to advertise their products. This can give a big boost to their bank accounts.

If you've got the talent, don't think you're too young to start dreaming of the Olympics. Teenage diver Tom Daley was thirteen years old when he competed at his first Olympic Games. He didn't win a gold medal then, but two years later at the age of fifteen Tom became a diving world champion.

Tips to make it to the top:
- **Concentrate – keeping your focus can help you to succeed.**
- **Stay positive – believe you can win.**
- **Practise – don't just rely on your talent to get you to the top.**
- **Stay motivated – join a local club or team to keep on improving your skills.**

If you follow these tips, you've got a great chance of becoming a sporting superstar.

GET CREATIVE

Want to find some creative ways to generate cash? If you're got a talent for music, art or writing, here are some ideas to get you started.

This section will help you on your way to:

- Writing a bestselling book
- Topping the charts with a hit song
- Making some cash by creating your own magazine
- Giving your bank account some comic ka-pow
- Taking photos to turn a profit
- Making money from your art

Right, it's time to write the next million-seller!

How to write a bestseller

Do the stories you write always get top marks in school? Why not try to use your storytelling skills to write a bestselling book? You could become the next J K Rowling! Follow these tips to find out how.

Get reading

Before you can become a great writer, you've got to be a great reader. Read as many books as you can to learn how other writers tell their stories.

Ask your friends which books they love to read and look at the books in the bestseller charts. Can you spot what makes them popular? Fantastic characters, gripping plots, but most of all, a stunningly original idea all help to turn a story into a top seller.

Get inspired

You need to decide what story you want to tell. Keeping a diary can help you to get inspired. Lots of authors get their ideas for books from things that happen in their everyday lives.

The idea for your story might start from just a little spark — a character or a scene that jumps into your mind, but if you feed the flame of your imagination you'll soon work out where you want the story to go.

This might be a thrilling adventure, a romantic fantasy or even just a story that makes people laugh.

Make sure your idea is an original one. Don't copy a story from a book or a film. Nobody wants to read a rip-off!

Get writing

Writing a book is like building a house — you have to build it one word at a time. Try to make time to write your book every day, even if it's just for a few minutes at a time. The children's author SC Ransom wrote her first novel using her mobile phone on her daily train journey to work. Could you start writing a novel on your trip to school?

Don't worry if you get writer's block. There might be times when you get stuck and don't know what to write next. Taking a break can help clear your head and when you come back to your story you'll find the right words. Stick at it and you'll soon be writing "The End".

True story of a bestselling author

When fourteen-year-old Christopher Paolini began writing a story about a boy who discovers a dragon's egg, he didn't realize that it would turn into a bestselling book. His fantasy novel *Eragon* has now sold millions of copies and even been turned into a Hollywood film.

Get published

Before you can see your story in your local bookshop, you need to find someone to publish it. Look at who publishes the books that you like and check out the publishers' websites for contact details.

Some publishers will only look at stories that are sent to them by literary agents. An agent is a talent-spotter who helps their authors find a publisher and takes a cut of the money they make. Before you send an agent or publisher your book, write a snappy letter or email telling them what the story is about and asking if they'd like to read it. If you don't, your book might end up in the bin without being read!

Make sure the manuscript is in the right format before you send it out. Type it in Word using a clear font like Times New Roman in 12 point size. Double space the text and indent the first line of every new paragraph. Remember to include your name and contact information on the first page of your manuscript, along with the title of the story. Then add your name, story title and page number at the bottom of every page.

If you're posting your story to a publisher, don't staple it — just use an elastic band instead. If you get a lot of rejections at first, don't give up. The first Harry Potter book was rejected more than a dozen times, but has now made millions for its author J K Rowling.

How to write a hit song

Fancy the life of a jet-setting pop star with screaming fans, fame and fortune? If you've got some musical talent, why not try writing a song that will make it to the top of the charts? Follow these steps to get started.

Step 1 – Make music

The best way to start writing a hit song is to just start playing. Strum your guitar, tinkle on a keyboard or even give a blast on the trumpet to try and create a new tune. Record yourself as you play to capture any flashes of inspiration. Play this back to try and spot what sounds good – this might be the start of a hit song.

Don't worry if you don't play a musical instrument. Nowadays you can use computer programs and apps like GarageBand to create and record a hit song. These programs have hundreds of sampled and synthesized instruments you can use to make your own music. Experiment and play around with sounds to try and create a chart-topping tune.

Step 2 – Make it catchy

Every hit song needs a hook. This might be a killer intro, an infectious melody or a chorus that you can't help singing along to. The biggest-selling hits will have all three!

Some people write the words to a song first, then create a melody to match them, whilst for other songwriters the tune comes first. Whichever way you choose, you need to write some lyrics that will stick in the mind.

Use rhyme to craft your verses and don't forget to focus on the chorus. This is the part of the song where you want everyone singing along. Keeping the chorus simple will help to make it catchy. Lots of popular songs have the following structure: verse / chorus / verse / chorus / bridge / chorus. The bridge is a new-sounding part of a song that leads back into the chorus.

Don't let your song wear out its welcome. Most hit songs are less than four minutes long. If you can keep your song short, you've got more chance of getting it played on radio and TV – this will help make it a hit.

142

Step 3 – Make it big

Once you've written your song, you need to make it a hit. Here are a few ways you could get your song heard.

• Sell your song to a top pop star – lots of famous singers work with teams of songwriters to create their hits. Send a copy of your song to the manager of your favourite pop star. If they like it, you might get to see them take it to the top of the charts!

• Enter a TV talent show – if you've got a great voice as well as a great song, this is a fantastic way to get your music heard by millions of people. If you can win the competition, all the fans that you make will rush out to buy your song.

• Get your song on YouTube – make a video of your song and post it online. 13-year-old Rebecca Black posted a video of her song "Friday" and got millions of hits in a week. The talent of the million-selling pop star Justin Bieber was also spotted first on YouTube.

How to create your own magazine

Take a look on the shelves of your local newsagent. You'll find magazines about everything under the sun: fashion, food and drink, music, video games, and much, much more. Making your own magazine can be a great money-spinner if you pick the right topic.

Market research

Who do you want to read your magazine? Do you want to aim it at people your own age? How about readers who have a particular hobby or interest? Or maybe you could make a magazine for everyone who lives in your local area? Whoever your audience is, you need to do some research.

Get together a group of your target readers. Ask them what magazines they already read. Find out their likes and dislikes. Do they want to read more interviews, features or reviews? What would they like to see in your magazine? Share your ideas and see what they think. The more you know about your readers, the better your magazine will be.

Look at other magazines you'll be competing with. How can you make your magazine different? Think of ways you can stand out from the crowd on the newsagent shelves. A snappy name for your magazine will help.

Get a team together

Most magazines are made by more than one person. You'll be the editor in charge, but you need a team of writers, designers and photographers to put your magazine together. Ask your friends if they want to help.

Brainstorm ideas for magazine features — these are the stories that will fill the pages of your magazine. Who could you interview? What could you review? Vote on the most popular choices, but remember that as the editor you have the final say. Give your team their jobs to do and get them started.

Sell ads for cash

Remember you want your magazine to make you money, so as well as features you need adverts to fill its pages. Find businesses that might want to advertise in your magazine. Tell them all about it and persuade them to put their adverts on its pages.

Remember to charge different prices for different sized ads. The most expensive should be the big advert on the back cover of your magazine. As you're launching a new magazine, you might want to discount the prices you charge to persuade people to advertise.

Get the layout right

You've got your articles ready, adverts filed and photos uploaded, but how do you turn all this into a magazine? You can use programs like Microsoft Publisher to help to create your magazine. This will let you lay out each page of your magazine – headlines, backgrounds, text, photos, captions – everything you see in a professional magazine. Remember to create an eye-catching design that will appeal to your readers.

Don't forget the front cover too. This should have a fantastic logo for the name of your magazine, a great image that will appeal to readers and snappy cover lines to tell them what's inside.

Launch your magazine

It's time to get your magazine on to the shelves. Decide on a price and work out how many you'll need to sell to make a profit. Remember to take into account how much it will cost to print your magazine. Talk to local newsagents and shops to see if they will stock your magazine before you start printing.

If all else fails, why not give your magazine away for free? This will get you a lot of readers. You can then make your money by charging more for the advertising space inside your magazine. You might soon have a million-seller!

How to make your own comic

Got a great idea for a new superhero who could beat up Batman? Maybe you've thought of a cartoon cat who's even funnier than Garfield. Writing and drawing a comic strip can be a creative way of earning some extra cash.

There are lots of different types of comics that you can create:

• Newspaper strips – these are the cartoons like Snoopy and Garfield that you find inside in a newspaper. They tell a funny story in three or four frames with the same characters appearing every day.

• Superhero comics – Spider-Man, Batman, Superman, the Hulk – there are hundreds of superheroes out there busily saving the world! Their adventures usually appear in comic books that come out every month.

• Funny comics – some comics like the *Beano* just want to make you laugh. The antics of different cartoon characters like Dennis the Menace appear on every page.

• Web comics – no, I'm not talking about Spider-Man again! These are comics that are published on the internet. They can be about anything – funny animals, geeky gamers, superhero stories – but most web comics tend to stick to telling a story in three or four frames like a newspaper strip.

How to make a cartoon strip

You will need:

- Blank paper
- A pencil
- A black felt-tip pen
- Coloured felt-tips
- A ruler
- A pencil eraser

1. First of all, you need to think of an idea for your cartoon strip. This might be the adventures of a useless superhero or even the funny things that your cat gets up to behind your back. Let your imagination run wild.

2. Now practise drawing the characters that will appear in your cartoon. Try to make each character instantly recognizable so that readers don't get them confused. Show how your characters feel by the expressions you show on their faces.

3. Work out how you will tell your comic strip story. Decide how many frames you will need. Note down what will happen in each one.

4. Now using the ruler and a black felt-tip pen, draw out the boxes for your cartoon strip on a piece of blank paper. Make the frames larger than the boxes in a newspaper strip — this will make it easier to draw. Don't worry — your comic strip can be shrunk to fit in a newspaper.

5. Using your pencil, sketch out the action in each frame. Remember to create a strong look for each character so your readers can tell them apart. Show how your characters feel by the expressions on their faces. Use motion lines to show action and movement.

6. Add any word balloons, thought bubbles and sound effects to your comic strip. Make sure you can read the letters — using capitals can help.

7. Now it's time to ink your comic strip. Take the black felt-tip and trace over your pencil sketches. Once the ink is dry, you can rub out your original pencil lines.

8. You might want to keep your cartoon black and white, but you can add colour as well. Use the other felt-tips to colour in your strip.

9. Now you need to find someone to buy your comic strip. Try sending a copy to the editor of your local newspaper and asking if they need a regular cartoon strip. That's how the comic creator Alan Moore got started and lots of his comics have now been made into Hollywood films.

10. If you can't find anyone to publish your strip, post it online as a web comic. Send your friends a link and ask them to pass it on to everyone they know. This can be a great way to get your comic strip out there and find lots of fans.

How to become a photographer

If you're handy with a camera, you might be able to make some money from the pictures you take. There are lots of people and places that need great photos and you could be the person to take them.

Right camera action!

Before you get started you need to make sure you've got the right equipment. If you want to see your photos appear in magazines or online, you'll need to take top-quality pictures. Use a digital camera that lets you take high-resolution photos. Lots of these cameras come with software to help you upload your pictures to a computer. You can then improve your photos with different effects.

Take pictures that sell

Look through magazines to find out what kind of pictures they use. You probably won't find many photos of your family, friends and pets, so don't think you can just start selling your snapshots!

Magazines, advertisements and websites all want unique images that have been shot in a stylish way. There are lots of different subjects you could photograph:

- Sporting scenes and action shots
- Pictures of people and places
- Photos of food and drink
- Interesting objects and funny situations
- Pictures that sum up special occasions like Christmas or Easter

Whatever subject you choose, there are websites that will sell your photos for you online. These are stock photo agencies which sell pictures to people who want to use them in adverts, magazines, brochures or websites. These agencies will only accept the very best photos so you'll need to make sure your pics pass the test.

How to take a great photo

Here are some handy hints to help you to get the best shots.

- Don't just snap away – plan the photos you want to take. Look through the viewfinder to carefully compose your picture. Think about what you want the photo to show.
- Make sure your photo is in focus. Nobody will want to buy a blurry snapshot for their magazine front cover.

• Get the right lighting. If you're taking photos outside, think about the time of day you take your picture in order to get the best light. Be careful with your flash if you're shooting indoors.

• If you take a picture with people in you'll need to get their permission first. Lots of photo agencies have release forms you can download and ask the people in your picture to sign.

• Keep your camera with you all the time in case you suddenly spot the perfect shot.

More money-spinning ideas

As well as selling your photos online, you can also sell your services as a top-notch picture-taker. Maybe your friends have started a band and need some publicity shots for their website. How about taking the photos at a family wedding? There are lots of occasions that need an official photographer and if you've got the skills it should be you.

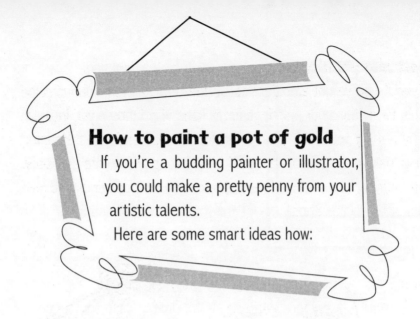

How to paint a pot of gold

If you're a budding painter or illustrator, you could make a pretty penny from your artistic talents.

Here are some smart ideas how:

Draw caricatures

Why not set up your drawing board at the school fair and start selling caricatures to people who pose for you? A caricature is an exaggerated portrait of a person – a bit like a cartoon. Maybe you'll make a big nose into a honking snout or a pointy chin into a triangle shape! A good caricature should be funny but not too cruel. Remember you want people to buy them!

Sell your paintings

Even if you've got ambitions to be the next Picasso, you won't be able to auction your paintings for millions of pounds — yet! Instead, why not try to exhibit your art in local shops and cafes. Hanging your paintings on its walls could brighten up a dull cafe and show off your art at the same time. Put prices on your paintings and give the owner of the shop a cut of the profits from any you sell.

Make pictures for your friends

If your friends are fans of your art, why don't you ask if they want to commission you? You could offer to draw or paint anything they like for a price. This might be a painting of a pet or a cartoon of their favourite pop star. You could even draw a portrait they could use as their profile picture on all their social networks.

If people try to haggle when buying your artwork, tell them they're getting a bargain. When you're a famous artist they'll be able to sell your art for hundreds of pounds!

THRIFTY LIVING

Be careful with your cash and avoid spending too much money by trying out these fun money-saving schemes – the more money you can save, the more you'll have to spend on things you really want!

This section will tell you how to:

- Save cash by customizing clothes
- Swap your way to some brand-new stuff
- Fix things to help you make and save money
- Recycle old printer cartridges to save you pounds
- Drive a hard bargain and pay the cheapest prices
- Find great deals and save yourself a fortune

First, check out a smart way to save some cash by revamping your old clothes.

How to customize clothes

If you want to stay on trend, you don't need to head out to the shops. Get a needle and thread and start hunting through your wardrobe instead. Customizing old clothes is a great way to bring old outfits back to life. Here are a few ideas to get you started.

• Button it! Take off boring old buttons and swap them for funky ones. You might find cool buttons on clothes you've grown out of or pick some up from charity shops.

• Sew cool! Transform old tops with a stitch or two. You can sew beads or sequins on to create a glittery new look or tie threads in knots to create an eye-catching pattern.

• Cutting-edge clothes! If your summer wardrobe looks a bit sparse, take a pair of scissors to your winter-wear. You can cut the legs off an old pair of jeans to turn them into shorts or chop a long-sleeved shirt into a vest!

• Frankenstein fashion! Take bits from different clothes to create a new item of clothing. You could turn the cuffs from an old jumper into fingerless gloves, a shirtsleeve into a scarf, or a school tie into a cool new belt.

If your friends say they like your customized clothes, help them to hunt through their wardrobes too. You could swap clothes to customize and start your own fashion trend!

How to swap what you want

You don't always have to pay out to get the best stuff. Why don't you try swapping things you don't need for the things that you want? That's what blogger Kyle MacDonald did when he traded in a red paperclip for bigger and better things until he got a house!

True story of a genius swapper

When Kyle posted a picture of a paperclip on his blog and asked if anyone wanted to swap, he didn't realize that less than year later he would have turned this paperclip into a place to live. The first person to swap with Kyle gave him a fish-shaped pen which he swapped again for a doorknob.

Kyle kept on swapping, travelling across Canada and the United States, getting bigger and better things each time: a camping stove, a snow mobile, even an afternoon with rock star Alice Cooper. His final swap turned a part in a Hollywood film into a two-bedroom house in the town of Kipling, Canada.

Swap shopper

So how can you swap your way to great new stuff? Make a list of the things you've got to swap (make sure they're yours and not your sister's!) and get your friends to do the same. Swap lists and write your names next to things you'd like. If you want something on your friend's list and they want something on yours, you've got a swap!

How to fix your way to a fortune

What do you do when something you own breaks? Do you just throw it away and buy a new one? If you try to fix things instead, you can save yourself money — and you might even make some extra cash, too.

What can you fix?

Don't think you can fix everything. It's not a good idea to start unscrewing the back of the washing machine if it floods the kitchen. Some repair jobs are best left to the professionals!

Here are some things that you can fix if you follow these tips.

• Gadget glitches — if your games console starts to freeze up, your digital camera won't take a picture or your mobile phone stops working, there's one thing you can try first. Turn it off and on again. 80% of gadget problems are fixed this way. If that doesn't work, check the power supply — you might need to change the battery.

• Decoration disasters — if the wallpaper's peeling or the garden fence is looking scruffy, a fresh lick of paint can make things look as good as new. You could sell your decorating services to your friends and neighbours — all you'll need is a paintbrush and a pot of paint.

• Fashion fixes — if your best party dress starts to split at the seams or the zip on your favourite jacket gets broken, don't panic. A needle and thread can soon fix any tears.

How to repair a broken zip

If the teeth on your zip come apart when you pull up the slider, use a small pair of pliers and a needle and thread to sort the problem.

1. First of all, pull off the metal stop from the bottom of the zip using the pliers.

2. Then pull the slider down to the bottom to allow you to get the teeth back into the right position.

3. Match them up one by one as you pull up the zip.

4. Finally, use your needle and thread to sew six or seven stitches at the bottom of the zip to make a new stop.

Your zip is back in full working order and it didn't cost you a penny!

How to recycle printer cartridges to save pounds

Does your printer keep on running out of ink? If buying new printer cartridges is putting a hole in your bank balance, why not recycle them instead? Here's how to refill an old cartridge with new ink so you can keep on printing. Make sure you get permission from whoever owns the printer first — and ask an adult to help you!

You will need:

- An ink refill kit (you can buy these from supermarkets or online)
- Kitchen roll
- Sticky tape
- A sharp pencil
- Plastic gloves (to protect your hands!)

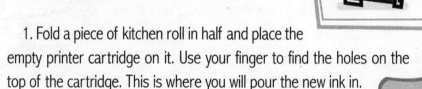

1. Fold a piece of kitchen roll in half and place the empty printer cartridge on it. Use your finger to find the holes on the top of the cartridge. This is where you will pour the new ink in.

2. Use the pencil to pierce the refill holes. The instructions that are included with the ink refill kit will help you to find the right holes. Depending on the type of cartridge you're filling, there will be a hole for the black ink or three holes for magenta, cyan and yellow if it's a colour cartridge.

3. Insert the needle of the refill ink bottle into the right hole. Make sure you push this all the way down into the bottom of the cartridge.

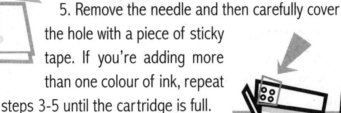

4. Now add the ink slowly. Make sure you don't spill any or overfill the cartridge. Stop filling as soon as any ink starts to come out of the top of the hole.

5. Remove the needle and then carefully cover the hole with a piece of sticky tape. If you're adding more than one colour of ink, repeat steps 3-5 until the cartridge is full.

6. Dab the cartridge printhead – this is where the ink comes out – on the paper towel to get the ink flowing. Make sure the cartridge isn't leaking before you put it back in the printer.

7. Print out a page to check that it's all working!

How to bargain at a market

You can't buy fleas at a flea market or car boots at a car boot sale, but you can bag a bargain! To get the best buys at the very best prices, you'll need quick wits, old clothes and a poker face.

Don't dress to impress

If you want to get a bargain, make sure you dress scruffy. Nobody will believe you can't pay full price if you turn up in designer clothes.

Find what you want to buy

The best bargain-hunters can spot a great deal in seconds. Keep an eagle eye out for any hidden treasures beneath the bric-a-brac.

Start negotiating

When you've found something that you want, it's time to haggle. Start low and offer about half the price the seller is asking for. They won't say yes straight away, but might ask for a little less than their original price. Keep making offers until you both agree on a price.

Keep your cool

The secret to bagging a bargain is not to show how much you want it. Keep a poker face and don't act too interested. Be polite, but don't talk too much — staying quiet might encourage the seller to make you a better offer.

Flash your cash

Showing the colour of your money can help you seal the deal. Pull out the exact money for the price you want to pay and tell the seller this is all the money you have. The sight of cash in your hand can convince them to sell. Make sure you take plenty of loose change.

And if you don't seal the deal...

Just walk away — they'll soon call you back if they really want to sell. There'll be more bargains out there on other stalls, but you'll need to be quick to beat any other bargain-hunters. You can always go back and try again at the end of the day. That's when sellers are desperate to shift their stock and you might get an even better deal!

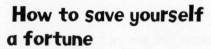

How to save yourself a fortune

Don't pay full price for anything that you buy! Turn yourself into a bargain-hunting machine to track down the best deals. Here are three great ways to save a ton of cash.

Get voucher spotting

Lots of shops give out money-off vouchers to tempt people to spend in their stores. You can sometimes find these vouchers in newspapers, but more often you'll find them online. Some websites like moneysavingexpert.com send out weekly emails to highlight the best vouchers on offer. These deals don't last for long, so you'll have to be quick to bag yourself a bargain.

You can also find vouchers for cheap cinema tickets, theme park rides and money off when you eat out in a fancy restaurant. Whatever you want to do, the chances are you'll be able to find a voucher if you look hard enough. Planning your social life around the vouchers you find can save you a packet!

Hit the sales

The best time to go shopping is in the sales. Follow these tips to help you bag a bargain.

• Before the sale starts, scope out store. Make a list of the things you'd like to buy if you spot them in the sale.

• On the day of the sale, set yourself a budget. Don't be tempted to spend more than this. If you can't afford it, it's not a bargain!

• Get there early. The best buys in a sale can be snapped up fast, so you'll need to be quick off the mark.

• If you don't want to get crushed in the crowds, curl up on the sofa with a computer and surf the sales instead. Lots of shops start their sales online, so you'll be first in the queue.

Find freebies

If you're bored but out of cash, there's tons of fun you can have for free. If you're looking for something to do, why not visit your local museum or art gallery? There will be lots of things to see and best of all it's probably free!

If you want a great book to read, pop along to your local library. You'll be able to borrow all the latest bestsellers free of charge. Why not download some free songs to listen to whilst you're reading your book? You can get free MP3s from music websites such as iTunes and Amazon and your favourite band might also let you download a song for free if you sign up to their website. You can play tons of fun computer games for free online and lots of video-game companies will let you download free demos of their latest games.

MONEY MATTERS

If you want to keep hold of your cash, you need to learn how to manage your money.

This section will tell you how to:

- Choose the right current account to look after the money you need every day
- Select the best savings account to make your money grow
- Manage your finances and keep to a budget
- Use credit and store cards sensibly
- Borrow money for the right reasons and pay it back
- Make sure you're paying the right amount of tax
- Make money from property
- Invest in stocks and shares
- Invest in a hedge fund and take risks with your cash
- Save for a pension to keep you comfortable when you're old and grey

Right, grab your cash — it's time to head to the bank!

How to choose the right current account

So where are you going to keep all the money you've made? Finding a safe place doesn't mean stuffing it under your mattress! You need to get yourself a bank account.

To open a bank account you'll need to fill in an application form. Take it along to the bank along with some proof of your ID (e.g. a passport) and where you live (e.g. a telephone bill). You might also need an introduction from your parents if they already bank there.

A current account is a bank account where you keep the cash you need for your everyday life. Current accounts can help you to manage your money as you'll be able to:

- Check your bank balance regularly to keep track of what you're spending
- Use a debit card to avoid paying with cash when you go shopping
- Pay for things using a cheque
- Get money in an instant from a cash machine

Debit cards and cheques:
A debit card looks like a credit card, but takes the money you spend straight out of your current account when you use it in a shop and key in your PIN number.

A cheque is a special piece of paper which you fill out to say who you want to pay and how much. The person then takes this cheque to their bank and the money comes out of your account two or three days later.

Always make sure you've got enough money in your current account before you use a cheque or debit card.

Choosing the right bank account isn't as easy as it sounds. Lots of banks will give you a free gift to try to tempt you into opening an account with them. This might be anything from a piggy bank to vouchers that give you money off activities and days out. Don't make the mistake of choosing your current account because of the gift you'll get – you need to keep an eye on the interest it pays, too.

Every account will pay you interest for the money you put in. How much interest they'll pay is shown as a percentage – this is called the interest rate. For example, if the interest

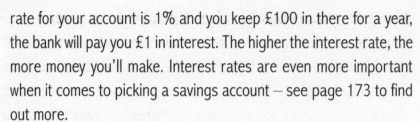

rate for your account is 1% and you keep £100 in there for a year, the bank will pay you £1 in interest. The higher the interest rate, the more money you'll make. Interest rates are even more important when it comes to picking a savings account – see page 173 to find out more.

Ask yourself these five questions to help you choose the best bank account:

- Does the bank have a branch in your area where you can go to pay your money in and ask for advice?
- Does the bank let you find out information about your account – i.e. how much money you've got – using a computer or mobile phone?
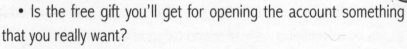
- Is the free gift you'll get for opening the account something that you really want?
- Does the bank give you any special offers such as free texts or music downloads when you use their cash machines?
- How much interest will you earn from the money in your bank account?

Finally, make sure you're the right age for the bank account you decide on.

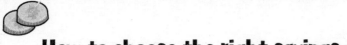

How to choose the right savings account

Saving money is an important skill. It can help you to get the things that you want — whether this is saving up for a new video game or putting money to one side for a great day out at a theme park. If you're a smart saver, you can make the money you save grow along the way.

The first thing you need to do is find a savings account. There are lots of different types of savings accounts, so you need to make sure you choose the one that suits you.

• Instant access accounts — this type of savings account lets you save as much or as little as you like and you can dip into your money whenever you want. If you've got some spare cash one month you can top up your savings, but if your Xbox breaks and you need to buy a replacement quickly then you can raid your account.

• Notice savings accounts — unlike instant access accounts, you need to give your bank warning before you can take your money out of a notice savings account. This might mean a wait of between 30, 60 or 90 days before you can lay your hands on your cash — but usually, this type of savings account gives you a better rate of interest than an instant access account.

• Regular savings accounts — if you want to save money every month, you could get yourself a regular savings account. You'll only be able to invest a set amount — this might be between £10 and £250, but you'll usually get a good rate of interest. However, this might not earn you as much money as you think. If you save £100 a month in a regular savings account that has a 10% interest rate, you'll only get £65.24 in interest not the £120 you'd expect if you deposited the money all at once. This is because you only get interest on your savings as they build up each month.

Depending on the type of account you choose, you'll either have a fixed or variable interest rate. A variable rate means the amount of interest you'll earn can go up or down depending on how the rate changes, but a fixed rate of interest gives you a guaranteed amount.

Don't dip into your savings every time you see something you want to buy. It's better to stick to your savings plan – you'll get what you really want in the end, and earn some interest too!

How to keep to a budget

Sticking to a budget helps you to stay in control of the money you spend. Follow these steps to work out your own budget.

1. First, work out how much money you earn in a year. This might include pocket money, money you earn from your money-making schemes and any birthday money.

2. Get a piece of paper and list where you get your money from and the amount you receive. Remember you want the annual amount, so if you get £5 pocket money a week times this by 52 to work out how much you get a year. Add this all up to find out your total annual income.

3. Now work out how much money you spend. Firstly think about any things that you have to spend money on — these might be bus fares to get to school or money for your lunch. Remember you want to find out how much you spend in a year, so get your calculator out to work this out. Write down each of these expenses.

4. Think about the other things that take care of your cash. This might be trips to the cinema, buying music downloads, or paying your mobile phone bills. Add all these to the list too. Now add up all your expenses to work out the total.

5. Do you spend more than you earn? If you do, you need to cut down on splashing out your cash!

6. Look down at your list of expenses. Is there anything you could stop buying or save money on? Be honest — think about what you really need, not just what you want.

7. Divide your total income by 52 to find out how much money you have to spend each week. This is your weekly budget and you can't spend more than this. Look down the list of your essential expenses and set yourself a spending target for each one. Make sure this doesn't go over your weekly budget.

8. Make a note of how much money you spend every week to make sure you're sticking to your budget. Don't get tempted by unexpected treats – make sure you can afford them before you start spending!

How to use a credit card

If you need to borrow money, you need to learn how credit cards work. Don't think that when you flash the plastic you're getting money for free. When you use a credit card you need to pay back everything that you borrow and some extra on top as well.

When you're under 18 years old, you can only get a prepaid credit card. This is a credit card that you load up with your own money and then when it's all spent you can't use the card any more. This stops you from getting into debt, but when you turn 18 this all changes. As a grown-up with a credit card you can borrow as much as you want – well, up to a limit that the credit card company sets – but you'll be charged interest every month on any money that you don't pay back straight away. Here's an example to show how it works:

• You buy yourself a brand-new video game console for £100 using your credit card.

• The annual interest rate on your credit card is 20%.

• This means that after one year the amount you have to pay back is £120. The £100 you've borrowed plus £20 interest.

• However, if you take two years to pay the money back, the amount you owe goes up. This is because in the second year you are charged another £20 interest on the money you originally borrowed (£100) and another £4 interest on the interest you were charged in the first year too. This means you now have to pay back £144!

The longer you take to pay your credit card off, the more money you'll be charged. Credit card companies are sneaky and only ask you to repay a minimum amount each month. If you do this, it will take you years to pay back what you owe. You'll end up being charged more in interest than the amount of money you originally borrowed!

Getting in debt can be frightening. You can lose everything you own, even your house, if you can't pay the money back. If you use a credit card, the best thing to do is pay back what you've borrowed as quickly as you can. This will save you money in the long run.

Some high street shops also offer their own type of credit cards. These are called store cards and often come with a special offer attached such as money off what you're buying if you sign up for a card. Beware! This might sound like a great deal, but store cards usually charge huge amounts of interest. This means any money you save can be wiped out by the interest you're charged. Don't be a sucker – steer clear of store cards!

How to borrow money and pay it back

Unless you were born rich or robbed a bank when you were a baby, it's almost impossible to go through life without borrowing money.

• If you want to buy a house, you'll need to borrow money – this kind of loan is called a mortgage.

• If you want to set up your own business, you might need to borrow money from an investor first.

• If you want to go to university, you'll need to borrow money to pay the fees the university charges to teach you.

Cash for qualifications

Many people take out student loans to pay for university. Even though it costs a lot of money, going to university can be good investment. People who have university degrees often earn more than those who don't, and you need a degree for many careers, including medicine, law and teaching.

A student loan isn't like an ordinary loan. You don't have start paying it back until you earn a certain amount of money. And if you haven't paid it back after a set number of years, the money you still owe is written off (so you don't have to repay it).

Whatever the reason you've got for borrowing, remember the three golden rules to stay out of money trouble.

• Only borrow money if it's really necessary. If you need money for a new bike because you can't get to school without one, that's a good reason to borrow. However, if you just want some cash to buy yourself a pony, that doesn't pass the test!

• Make sure you can afford to pay back the money that you borrow. Look at the interest rate and work out how much you'll need to pay back every month. Remember, the quicker you pay back the money that you owe, the less you'll have to pay in interest.

• Don't ever borrow more money to pay off your debts! This will get you into a vicious circle and you could end up with nothing at all. Stay in control of your borrowing – don't let your debts control you.

Your bank can also let you borrow money from your current account. This is called an overdraft. However, if you borrow too much or can't pay it back, the bank will charge you more money. The more money they charge you for being overdrawn, the more that you'll owe and it can be really tricky to pay it all back. You should only use an overdraft in an emergency if you're sure you can pay the money back the next month.

A taxing issue
So you've made your first million. You're wondering whether to spend it all on a solid-gold helicopter or a diamond encrusted Wii, when you realize – you haven't got a million pounds at all! You've had to pay some of your money in tax.

Tax is money you have to pay to the government. Once you start earning a certain amount of money, you start paying a percentage of your earnings in income tax, which the government spends on running the country. Your tax money pays for things like schools, transport, hospitals, pensions and helping support people who aren't able to work. Depending on where you live, you also pay council tax, which goes towards services like doctors, schools and keeping streets clean in your local area.

You might not think you pay taxes yet – but every time you buy a computer game, or an ice-cream, you pay tax to the government. This kind of tax is called Value Added Tax – VAT – and you automatically pay it on almost everything you buy. You don't have to pay VAT on books or children's clothes, though – or on food the government thinks is "essential". Strangely, the government counts ordinary biscuits as essential, but chocolate-covered biscuits as a luxury. So if you want to save your pennies, go for the plain digestives…

How to make money from bricks and mortar

You might think a house is just somewhere to live, but buying property can be a great money-making investment too. That's what brothers Philip and Mark Stewardson found out.

True story of two property tycoons

Philip and Mark started out by buying a grotty terraced house in Birmingham for £19,000. They spent £6,000 doing it up and then sold it for £32,000 – giving them a £7,000 profit. This gave them both a taste for house hunting and over time they bought 120 homes which are worth around £16 million! Philip and Mark rent out the homes they own and make a tidy profit every month.

How to buy a house

Somewhere to live is something worth saving for when you get older. Most people also need a mortgage to help them to buy a house. A mortgage is a special loan that you get from a bank or building society. You have to pay interest on the money you've borrowed and repay the mortgage bit by bit every month. You usually have 25 years to pay all the money back. If you get into trouble and can't afford to repay, the bank can take your house away!

How to invest in stocks and shares

If you want to make big bucks, you need to learn how to invest in the stock market. Here's a beginner's guide to get you started.

What is the stock market?

The stock market is a place where stocks and shares in companies like Coca-Cola are bought and sold.

What are stocks and shares?

A stock is a share of ownership in a company. If you buy stock in Coca-Cola, you are a shareholder – this means you own a slice of the company. This slice can be large or small depending on how many shares you buy.

Why buy stocks and shares?

To make money of course! The price of shares in different companies can go up and down. Clever investors look to buy shares at a low price and then sell it later at a higher price. An investor might hold on to their stock for days, months or even years, to try and sell at the best price to make a profit.

What are the risks?

Like I said, the price of shares can go up and down. When you decide to sell your

shares in a company, you'll only get what they're worth at that very moment. If this is less than the price you paid when you bought them, you'll lose money!

How can I make lots of cash?

The trick is only to invest in a company if you think the price of their shares is going to go up. You'll need to study the company's share price carefully before you buy. Is it going up every day, holding steady or falling fast? You can find information about the share prices in newspapers or online.

What's the catch?

You have to be 18 or older to buy stocks and shares. But that doesn't stop you from getting some practise in first...

1. Pick five companies that you want to invest in. You could pick companies you already know, like the brand of your favourite fish fingers, or you could have a look in a newspaper or on the internet and pick companies which are doing well in the stock market at the moment.

2. Decide how many shares you want to buy of each company, and work out how much that would cost you.

3. Follow the prices of your shares for the next seven days. At the end of the week, work out if your shares are worth more or less than the price you "bought" them for.

4. You could have a competition with your friends to see who makes the most money.

How to take risks with your cash

When you get older and are looking for places to invest the millions that you've made, you might want to try and get even richer by making a high-risk investment.

What is a high-risk investment?

A high-risk investment is a money-making scheme that could make you a huge amount of cash if it all goes right. If it goes wrong though, you will lose all the money you've invested. That's why this type of investment is usually made by people who are already rich as they can afford to take the risk. Sometimes these people will join together to form an investment club called a hedge fund.

How does a hedge fund work?

The members of a hedge fund pool their money together to invest in anything that will make them lots of money. This might be stocks and shares, precious metals like gold and silver, art and antiques, or even starting up a new company.

One person is put in charge of the hedge fund and he or she decides what to invest the money in. This person will get a percentage of any profits the hedge fund makes. The riskier the investment the more money they could make, but they could also lose a lot too. Running a hedge fund isn't a job for the faint-hearted!

What if it goes wrong?

Sometimes a risky investment can go terribly wrong. In 2007 a firm called Terra Nova paid £4.2 billion to take over EMI, the music company behind pop stars such as Katy Perry and Kylie Minogue. However, Terra Nova had borrowed money from a bank to help them make the deal and when three years later they couldn't pay it back, the bank took over EMI instead and Terra Nova lost all the money they'd invested.

If you're ever looking for a high-risk investment, make sure that you trust the person in charge. You'll be giving them millions of your own money, so you don't want them running off with your cash!

How to stay rich when you're old and grey

You might not worry about it now, but where will you get your cash from in your old age? You're going to need a pension if you want to splash out on some antique Playstation games to play in your retirement home!

What is a pension?

A pension is money that you are paid after you stop working and retire. You have to save for a pension before you get old or else you'll end up with very little money to live on. You can start saving from the day you are born and more than 60,000 children have started saving for their pensions already! The only catch is that you can't get at this money until you're 55.

How to save

The earlier you start saving for your pension, the more money you'll have when you're old and grey. Every £1 you save now will be worth more in your retirement than £1 you save when you're nearly 50 years old. This is because your pension earns interest as you save.

Let's have a look at how this works:

• If you pay £2,880 into a pension every year, the government will top this up with an extra £720 giving you a total of £3,600.

• The interest you earn on the money you put in will give an extra boost to your pension pot. If you keep on saving at the same rate with a 6% interest rate, you'll end up with a pension worth nearly £2 million by the time you retire.

GET MONEY MAKING

You've read the book — now you need to put these money-making ideas into action. Think about which schemes you want to try first, and don't forget to look for ways to save money too. A clever money-maker should always be smart when it comes to spending their own cash. Now, get out there and start making your first million!